GATHERING
THE
CLOUDS

Clouds of Witnesses Who Will Strengthen Your Faith

Enoch Thweatt, Jr.;
Jeannine Thweatt

LifeRich Publishing is a registered trademark of The Reader's Digest Association, Inc.

LifeRich Publishing books may be ordered through booksellers or by contacting:

LifeRich Publishing
1663 Liberty Drive
Bloomington, IN 47403
www.liferichpublishing.com
844-686-9607

New International Version (NIV)

ISBN: 978-1-4897-3196-8 (sc)
ISBN: 978-1-4897-3195-1 (hc)
ISBN: 978-1-4897-3197-5 (e)

Library of Congress Control Number: 2020922511

Print information available on the last page.

LifeRich Publishing rev. date: 11/23/2020

CONTENTS

CLOUD ONE
That Great Cloud of Witnesses

CLOUD TWO
That Great Cloud of the Prophets of Israel

CLOUD THREE
That Great Cloud of the Messianic Prophets

CLOUD FOUR
That Great Cloud of the Victories of Jesus

CLOUD FIVE
That Great Cloud of Evidence from the Empty Tomb

CLOUD SIX
That Great Cloud of Living Witnesses of a Risen Messiah

DEDICATION

There are many people who have influenced us for good throughout our long lives, and we are very much obligated to them for their loving guidance. It would be difficult to choose one over another for this honor. However, the nature of this study compels us to consider someone else.

Who is the Word that became flesh two thousand years ago? Who came and lived among the people of this earth? Who came in humble obedient faith and love to offer Himself *for my sins and yours,* as a sacrifice to God? It is God who is the Word that became flesh, born in a stable, raised as the son of a carpenter, facing all the temptations we face, yet remaining sinless – *His name is Jesus.*

Therefore,

***Gathering the Clouds* is dedicated to**

Jesus,

the Author and Finisher of our faith.

Enoch B. Thweatt, Jr.

and

Jeannine P. Thweatt

NOTE: Book Two of *A Trilogy of Clouds* is entitled *Beware the Dark Clouds.* It is a study of the struggle between right and wrong, good and evil, justice and injustice. All people on earth are involved in this struggle – some strongly active for the right, for the good, and for justice; some barely active either way; and some strongly active for the wrong, for the evil, and for injustice. God has given each one of us the responsibility to choose which side of the struggle to be on. An examination of the ways of the Evil One will be made and exposed; everyone will be encouraged to seek God's help to be victorious in these *very personal daily battles.*

Book Three is entitled *The Clouds of Glory.* It is a study of the good works God planned in advance for His people to do (Ephesians 2:10). From this study, one will come to realize the indescribable joy of serving others as we do His good works.

PREFACE

A few years ago, Enoch felt the need to understand several topics more deeply but had no plan to do any research. But one event led to another: first, a need to write a short booklet; second, a need to understand how Christians relate to Abraham today; third, a need to understand true repentance as Jesus taught; fourth, a need to become truly involved and faithful to God all the time; fifth, a need to understand and become a part of what Jesus continues to build. All of these topics required additional thoughtful, diligent study. After eight months, the results overwhelmed him; he knew he had to share what to him was very valuable information. But how? And with whom?

As he began to write and share with a few good friends, one of them asked him, *Enoch, who is your target audience?* After thinking about it, he realized the answer was *ME, Myself!* He was not preparing to teach a class, or preach a sermon, or speak at some retreat; he was studying for his own edification and learning.

That changed everything. Enoch began to write about what, he soon realized, were many passages that strengthened his own faith. Thus, **Gathering the Clouds** had its birth, but it also needed to go through what we call its adolescent period. After an opportunity to teach much of the young, immature, first edition, the response and input from our Bible class students indicated that it needed more "maturing." The result is the first book in **A Trilogy of Clouds.**

More than fifty Christians read various chapters and made many excellent suggestions which we have gratefully incorporated into the final revision.

Reading to give our own faith a boost can also become a means of sharing God's love with family members, and others. *Let the texts do the teaching and generate faith* (or strengthen it). Let our comments be a help along the way. Our task is to **let the texts of God's Word, God's Truth, do its powerful work and encourage our own faith to grow.**

These texts will bring all believers closer to Jesus in mind and heart, with a serendipity: It will draw all believers closer to each other spiritually. That is what Jesus died for – *that we all would be one in Him as He and the Father are One!* (John 17).

Enoch and Jeannine Thweatt

PROLOGUE

Cloud One, the image of a *Great Cloud of Witnesses,* in Hebrews 11, made us realize there are at least five other *Great Clouds* which can be found in the scriptures. **Cloud Two** concerns *The Prophets of Israel,* whose words most of which came true shortly after they were spoken. **Cloud Three** examines *The Prophets of the Messiah*, about whom many books have been written. *The Victories of Jesus* make up **Cloud Four;** in all of those victories no blood was shed, no physical battle was fought. **Cloud Five** emphasizes *The Testimony of the Empty Tomb,* a powerful message the whole world needs to know. **Cloud Six** expresses the testimony of *The Living Witnesses of the Risen Messiah,* **whose blood was shed in** *His Conquering of sin and death.*

These witnesses testified to the **reality of the resurrection** of Jesus. They are our compelling personal witnesses; Jesus is the Risen Christ! He came to save all people, Jews and Gentiles, all languages, all skin colors, all communities on earth.

Let us urge all readers not to read this book quickly like a novel, but to read carefully, thoughtfully, **absorbing the texts. Allow God's Truth** to strengthen your faith. When a married couple spends time reading together, discussing the words and actions of these people of obedient faith, their trust in God will grow. So will their relationship to one another grow. May the power of these Biblical texts strengthen our own faith.

The witnesses in Hebrews 11 are actually those who were running the race of life in a way pleasing to God. They are our good examples; we watch them run their race.

God calls each of us to run our own race, not against fellow Christians, but against the temptations and deceptions of the Evil One. Why not *put on the sandals of those we will be reading about and run with them?*

The world has had to deal with false witnesses since human beings first lived on this earth. The witnesses we are studying are testifying to the truth. Our references to the Judge are like a prayer request to God to help us write in harmony with His will.

To help us think concretely about these events, we have used a courtroom scene, **but it is not a trial type with a jury.** It is more of a *hearing* where the evidence is laid out for everyone to consider. It is this kind of understanding that grows our own faith. To set the stage for what is to follow, we use the **Judge**, who is to see that we present the evidence clearly and fairly, and to tell **Me** how to proceed. The **Bailiff** is the court officer responsible for carrying out the **Judge's** instructions and for calling witnesses.

Please do not let any of these helpful (we hope) devices distract us from God's Holy message. Finally, it is up to us, as students of the evidence, to judge each passage, weigh the evidence, and accept its truth into our own hearts.

Enoch B. Thweatt, Jr. Jeannine P. Thweatt

GATHERING THE CLOUDS

BOOK ONE OF
A TRILOGY OF CLOUDS

In the beginning of Hebrews 12, the writer considers all those mentioned in chapter 11 as **A Great Cloud of Witnesses.** We need to listen to their testimony. There are five other clouds we need to examine to give our own faith a real opportunity *to keep on growing stronger.*

CHAPTER ONE

Evidence from the Created Universe,

Abel, Enoch, Noah, Abraham, Sarah

The Judge has entered the courtroom
to hear the evidence.
Me: *Your Honor, we propose to present something
about each of the witnesses mentioned as a part of
That Great Cloud of Witnesses in Hebrews, chapter 11,
but there are several other clouds
which we also need to present.*
Judge: *Understood, but let us take the
Clouds one group at a time. Bailiff,
announce the first Witness from Hebrews, chapter 11.*

Bailiff: *The Created Universe*

Judge: *I have a question. How do you propose to make
the Created Universe a Witness?*
Me: *Your Honor, we offer the Universe itself because it
proclaims its existence for all to see everywhere.*
Judge: *Very well. Bailiff, please call
each witness as appropriate.*

Bailiff: *Please present the Evidence for*
The Created Universe
Me: *Thank you, Bailiff. Let us begin by*
recognizing what the text reveals.

Something awesome took place that cannot be explained or even proven in anyone's laboratory. What tremendous power put the universe in such an amazing harmony! Creation does not take place in a test tube, and it does not take place in a fusion lab. Hebrews 11:2 tells us that it came about at God's command. That verse also tells us that what we can see with our eyes was made from something that cannot be seen by human eyes.

The elements hydrogen and oxygen in their basic form cannot be seen with the human eye. Combined, they form water. Water can be seen as a liquid, or as steam, or as ice. But in its gaseous state, we call it humidity; it cannot be seen. Thousands of pages could be written about various other elements to illustrate this phenomenon, but that misses the main point. The marvel of creation is the source of all those "unseen" elements that became "seen" things in the universe. This huge universe of which all mankind is a part exists. It is real, extremely complex, marvelously inter-dependent, and the small part of the universe in which we live is quite suitable for life to survive and flourish. All of us experience this reality every day whether we recognize it or not.

Almost every person who lives on this earth, or who has ever lived on this earth, has had the opportunity to observe all kinds of things every day all around where he lives. Paul said that, since the beginning, mankind has been able to see the *invisible attributes of God*. The eternal power of the Creator is undeniable and can be verified by looking at *what has been made* – and all people everywhere can see for themselves. This makes it possible to recognize that there has to be an Intelligent Planner, a Power – a Creator. This leaves no excuse

2

for anyone who fails to see the clear evidence from the things that have been made.

Wherever you go on the earth you will find people paying homage in one form or another to the natural aspects of this marvelous universe. The apostle Paul, in Romans 1:20, states emphatically that all of us on the earth have **no excuse!** The reason for this statement should be obvious: *we can all see for ourselves!* This witness is available for all people in all parts of the world, and *the message is the same.* The awesome complexity of the Universe, especially all life forms, makes it quite unreasonable to even think about the universe creating itself!

David wrote these words that truly challenge our thinking.

Psalm 19:1 – 2

1 The heavens declare the glory of God;
the skies proclaim the work of his hands.

2 Day after day they pour forth speech;
night after night they reveal knowledge.

How can the heavens **declare** (inform, pour forth, keep telling) the **glory** (honor) of God? How can the **skies** (firmament, sky above, horizon) **proclaim** (declare, reveal, announce) **the work of His hands** (craftsmanship, handiwork)? David complicates the answers to these questions by stating that they **pour forth speech** day by day, and **reveal knowledge** night after night – but they cannot speak (with a voice); they have no words to use; they cannot make an intelligible sound. **But they still communicate!**

Their message, though not verbal, spreads out to all the earth, to every "corner" of our globe. The earth was created for people, and we need to recognize the silent voices of this marvelous creation. The flowers speak, but not in an audible

3

language. How do the tides communicate? By what they do! The thunder and lightning, and even the rain, all make noises, but not in a human language. Their message is understood by observing what they do. All creation speaks a language we can "hear" with our eyes, our sense of smell, taste, and touch – all for the good of mankind.

The Creator intended for mankind – people, all kinds of people – to take control of the earth and rule over all living things: the fish in the sea, the birds in the sky, and everything that lives on the face of the earth (Genesis 1:27 – 28).

It is true: *every living creature* proclaims its own marvelous and amazing story. The inter-dependence of these life forms is intricate and complicated far beyond our normal understanding. Some people have spent their lives studying just one life form. In some cases, the result testifies that this inter-dependence with other life forms makes it impossible for the forms to have created themselves.

The same can be said for the celestial part of the universe. The attraction of one heavenly body to all other planets, stars, moons, and galaxies is what holds it all together. The centripetal and centrifugal forces, along with the "simple" law of gravity, operate the same throughout all the known galaxies, producing a universe which functions in an orderly manner. These forces also hold the earth and moon in an elliptical path as they travel around the sun. What a witness is the created universe, displaying the omnipotence of the Creator!

The apostle Paul also gave us information about the universe that scientists today are learning more and more about. First, he stated that the flesh of humans, animals, birds, and fish are all different. Then he stated that the different kinds of heavenly bodies have their own measure of brightness, the same being true of earthly bodies. Our sun and the stars all generate light and radiant energy, but the moons simply reflect the light that comes to them (I Corinthians 15:39 – 41).

What did Paul know about the universe? Was he a physicist or an astronomer? He was neither, but this is evidence that this information came from the Spirit of the Creator, not from within Paul himself.

We can observe the difference in the brilliance of the stars with our own eyes, even without a telescope. Sometimes one star will appear to be brighter than another, but with a strong telescope, we can learn that the brighter star may actually be much closer to the earth, making it appear more brilliant. Our sun is a very small "star" when compared to all the other stars, but it gives the earth just the right amount of radiant energy, and has been doing this since it was created. The splendor of the sun comes from that radiant energy and light, vital for human life. This is one way God has blessed all life on earth. Too much heat or not enough, and life on earth would be impossible.

The earth's moon has a different kind of splendor. It does not create light or heat for the earth, nor does it rotate on its axis. From the earth, we cannot see the far side of the moon, but we can see its face which reflects the sun's light to the earth. But the moon's splendor is much more than its reflected light.

Look at what we know. The entire universe is enormous, but very few people have the opportunity to study it through powerful telescopes. However, many of us can look through our own ordinary telescopes and learn much about our part of the universe: the sun, its planets, and their moons. What holds them together in their respective places? We know our solar system, as all heavenly bodies, moves through space, yet remains in the same relationship to the rest of the universe. Let us focus on our sun, our earth, and its moon, and recognize what we do know. There is an amazing phenomenon we can all see for ourselves.

The earth travels in an ellipse around the sun in approximately 365.25 days. The moon travels around the earth about fifty-eight times every thirty days. What keeps the earth and the moon in their orbits year after year? How can the sun, being about 93 million miles away from the earth, have any power to hold the earth and all its other planets in their respective orbits? The mass of the sun is thousands of times greater than the mass of the earth, and the mass of the earth is fifty times greater than the mass of its moon. Understanding this helps us realize how powerful this force is. It is able to keep these attractions in balance, perhaps forever. Without this balance, neither the earth nor its moon could be held in its orbit. Though difficult to study and know, that is part of the splendor of the moon and the entire universe.

There is another splendor we can all see. The moon travels around the earth in twelve hours and twenty-five minutes, or about twice each day. But how does that explain the splendor that Paul was talking about? Each time the moon travels around the earth, the attraction of one heavenly body to another brings an amazing blessing to our earth – *the tides wash all the shores of the earth two times each day!* Without the tides, all the refuse brought down to the shores by inland rivers would stay at the river mouths, and the buildup of filth would be unbearable! Anyone can see this on any seashore and behold the splendor of God's creation. Can we also see the loving care God had for people, *even as He planned the creation*?

Many animals eat only various grasses or plants, while humans enjoy all kinds of delicious foods. Fruits, vegetables, grains, nuts, meats, and seafood for example, were planned, at the beginning of creation, as a healthy diet for all people to enjoy. Is this not another way God shows His love for all human beings? Another book would be inadequate to express the extent of God's love for man as He created everything.

David's eighth Psalm contains several descriptions of the sovereignty of God – *how majestic is your name in all the earth!* (v. 1). Verse 6 tells about the responsibilities for mankind in God's creation plan – *You made them rulers over the works of your hands*. Verse 9 reveals a secret about the

6

existence of ocean currents and pathways for – *all that swim the paths of the seas.* And with David we also sing,

> LORD, *our Lord, how majestic is*
> *your name in all the earth!*

The Bible often refers to God as the Creator of the earth, sun, moon, and stars. The Bible also contains many teachings about the role of mankind, including man's responsibilities toward all other life forms. The natural earth on which we live and all the universe itself are powerful testimonies of an omnipotent, an omniscient, and an omnipresent Creator.

In ancient times, all written materials were done by hand. Then came type setting, movable type for mass printing, typewriters and their operators. Superior typists have been able to type at more than one hundred words per minute. But in this high tech age, this document for which we are now in the process of final revision, has more than 69,000 words; it can be copied and saved to a folder in less than two seconds. What is the point, you may ask? The point is: man has been discovering many things about our created universe for thousands of years, but *we are only discovering, not creating!* The ability found in micro-chips was discovered, not built into it by the discoverer. This is amazing testimony to the Omniscient Creator of our universe.

This Psalm not only harmonizes with the charge God gave to mankind in Genesis 1:28, but also introduces a physical concept that was not understood by mankind until the last several centuries. The expression in verse 8, *all that swim the paths of the seas*, must have seemed strange to the original readers of the Psalms.

In the spring of 1945, Enoch was a young third-class petty officer operating sonar equipment searching for German submarines in Atlantic waters. When he got a very strong contact signal about two or three thousand yards away, he continued, as was standard procedure, to determine the size of the contact. When it turned out to be several miles long, he knew it could not be a submarine. It was the Gulf Stream, one of the paths of the sea! (Yes, it was his first trip across the Atlantic, and the officers were watching to see what he would do with such a big target!). Since that day he has had the privilege of crossing the Pacific by ship two times, the Indian Ocean once, and the Atlantic a third time. He knows first hand; there are many paths in the seas of our earth's oceans. But how did the Psalmist know?

The testimony of the universe as a witness is amazing, mind-boggling, humbling, and consistent: **God created the universe and all of its inanimate and living parts.**

○ ○ ○ ○ ○

Bailiff: *Please present the evidence for*

Abel, Son of Adam

Me: *Thank you, let us examine*

Hebrews 11:4

*By faith Abel brought God a better
offering than Cain did.
By faith he was commended as righteous,
when God spoke well of his offerings.
And by faith Abel still speaks, even though he is dead.*

The difference in the gifts of Cain and Abel is explained in Genesis 4:4. Abel made a better offering (a fat one) from the firstborn of his flock. Human beings make their own decisions about what is better for certain purposes. By inference, Abel thought about what he wanted to give to God, and decided to give his best, while Cain did not seem to think that way. Does it not become clear that the difference is in the attitude of heart of these two brothers? God saw that Abel was truly grateful, but evidently saw something lacking in Cain. There is no record of God giving them a command to offer anything. What Abel did is a kind of witness that speaks very loudly to all of us today.

We need to ask ourselves two questions. *Do I offer to God from the best of the blessings I have received?* Or, *Do I give to God only what I have left over?* The very strong inference is that Cain did not offer the best he had. The problem did not come from the offering itself, but from the lack of sincere gratitude from the heart of Cain.

Is not what Abel did, by choosing the best, an appreciation for what God had done for him? No wonder that the Hebrew writer praises his testimony which remains with us thousands of years later! Abel definitely is an example of how we can show our appreciation to God for His blessings by what we give and what we do for other people.

Matthew expresses how God blesses all people in chapter five.

Matthew 5:44 – 45

44 But I tell you, love your enemies and
pray for those who persecute you,

45 that you may be children of your Father in heaven.
He causes his sun to rise on the evil and the good,
and sends rain on the righteous and the unrighteous.

The blessings of sunshine and rain come to even the poorest of people on this earth. It does not matter whether they are good or evil, just or unjust; those blessings are for all people. On this matter, God daily shows that He does not discriminate. Our task is to recognize the blessings we do have, choose the best and offer it to God. Abel distinguished himself by choosing to offer the fat of his flock, a marvelous example for us. His example lives on, many, many years after his death!

o o o o o

Bailiff: *Please present the evidence for*

Enoch, Who Pleased God

Me: *Thank you, let us examine*

Hebrews 11:5

By faith Enoch was taken from this life, so that he did not experience death: "He could not be found, because God had taken him away." For before he was taken, he was commended as one who pleased God.

We do not know much about this witness, but what we do know is certainly a great example for us. Enoch was commended because he lived his life to please God. What he did was by faith and trust in God. The first two human witnesses did what they did because they put their trust in God. How important is it for us today to put our full trust in God? The Hebrew writer makes it very plain that we cannot please God without faith. God rewards those believers who are searching for Him (Hebrews 11:6).

How do we know that the lives of both Abel and Enoch pleased God? Is it not by what they did from the heart? That is why it is very important to understand that our own true faith will be obvious to those around us when we live obediently to the God that we trust. We want to please God each moment of our lives. At the same time, we must do our best to refrain from those things that displease Him! It is not just *saying* that we believe in God; it is *doing* what we say we believe. The testimony of Enoch is strong because he lived his whole life in complete trust in God.

o o o o o

Bailiff: *Please present the evidence for*

Noah, Who Built the Ark

Me: *Thank you, let us examine*

Hebrews 11:7

By faith Noah, when warned about
things not yet seen, in holy fear
built an ark to save his family. By his
faith he condemned the world
and became heir of the righteousness
that is in keeping with faith.

It took Noah 100 years to complete the building of that huge boat. Why did he do it? God had warned him that all people on the earth, except Noah's own family, were so evil that He planned to flood the earth and destroy them all. This struck fear in the heart of Noah, who trusted God and also loved his family. How strong was Noah's faith in God? It was so strong that even when he was 500 years old he began building a boat on dry land. This goes against all "common sense" for us today. But it illustrates clearly what real faith and trust in God are all about. This trust did not waiver for the 100 years it took to build that huge structure. Are we paying attention to this witness as an example for our own faith today?

There are other things to learn from this man who trusted God as opposed to the tide of all the others living at that time. What did God see in the people around Noah?

Genesis 6:5

The LORD saw how great the
wickedness of the human race
had become on the earth, and that
every inclination of the
thoughts of the human heart was only evil all the time.

We do not know anything about how close, or far away, the neighbors of Noah lived. We do not know anything about his neighbors, except they were all evil. Noah and his family walked in righteousness in the presence of God. He did not succumb to the temptations of his evil neighbors.

Understanding the environment in which Noah lived, or wearing his sandals during that 100 years of "boat building," reveals an example of living with a complete trust in God that is worthy of prayerful thought by all believers today. Enoch recently observed his 94th birthday and he finds it very difficult to even consider spending his whole life building a boat on dry land! When he thinks about what it would be like to be "on the ground" with Noah for those 100 years, he realizes that Noah was a patient man, a persevering man, a true family man, a caring man, and a man of unwavering faith and trust in God. Our faith is strengthened when we think deeply about Noah. The full story is recorded in Genesis 6 – 9. Let Noah's faith strengthen your faith!

o o o o o

Bailiff: *Please present the evidence for*

Abraham, the Father of the Faithful

Me: *Your Honor, there is much to learn*
from this witness, both from

*Hebrews 11 and from other Old Covenant
passages, and it is vital for us
today. If you please, may the Bailiff present
each section as appropriate?*
Judge: *That is a reasonable request
and is granted. Bailiff, please
call each section as so requested.*

Bailiff: *Please present the evidence for*

God Called; Abraham Listened and Obeyed

Me: *Thank you. Let us begin by examining*

Hebrews 11:8 – 10

*8 By faith Abraham, when called to
go to a place he would later
receive as his inheritance, obeyed and went,
even though he did not know where he was going.*

*9 By faith he made his home in the promised land
like a stranger in a foreign country;
he lived in tents, as did Isaac and Jacob,
who were heirs with him of the same promise.*

*10 For he was looking forward to
the city with foundations,
whose architect and builder is God.*

By faith Abraham . . . obeyed and went. These six words
are an independent clause in verse 8 above. The dependent
clause in the middle of the verse reveals what motivated him
to obey. The Greek language reveals the order of the original
ideas, as follows: *By faith, when he was called, Abraham
obeyed to go out to a place which he would receive as*

13

an inheritance; (and) **He set out even though he did not know where he was going.** Think about what God was calling Abraham to do. Abraham had to have tremendous trust in God in order to obey that call from God!

When we moved from Nashville to Memphis over five years ago, we brought a lot of furniture, books, tools, patio stuff, and who knows what else. But we also had friends to help us load it all, family members to help drive the big trucks we conveniently rented, and accomplished it all in a few days. We felt it was a big task, but what about Abraham with all that he had to move more than a thousand miles?

It is about 500 miles from Ur to Haran, and almost 400 miles from Haran to the promised land, that is, if you could walk a straight line. But they followed the Euphrates River to Haran, and it does not flow in anything like a straight line. They did not have a river to follow from Haran to the promised land, but they had many mountains, streams, and valleys to cross. No straight line there either! What a contrast there is in moving a household today, and the move Abraham had to make.

In our own minds, let us walk along with Abraham and his family with all of their possessions, flocks of sheep, herds of cattle, food for the livestock, and much more. And, they are moving to **a place they had never seen!** Can we grasp the obedient faith of Abraham? Time passed slowly as they traveled, but Abraham's trust in God remained strong. Following his example can inspire confidence that *our own faith can grow stronger.*

Among this **Great Cloud of Witnesses,** Abraham shines very brightly. It was many years before Abraham actually arrived in the "promised land." But when he arrived, and settled in the land, he lived in it *like a stranger in a foreign country.*

Years ago we lived among a people we did not know. They spoke a language we could not speak, and their customs we did not understand. We truly felt like strangers, for a while. But as we learned to speak their language and develop friendships – friendships that have lasted more than sixty years – we no longer felt like strangers. Even to this day we have close ties with these friends. Is this what Abraham experienced? We know his name did become great, indicating that he had the respect of the people among whom he lived. But what about his *living like a stranger in a foreign country?* There must be a deeper meaning.

Christians live in this world, but must not make that life the goal for eternity. We are not to be *of this world,* meaning that there is a deeper purpose for our lives than just acquiring wealth, or status, or power. The promise God made to Abraham included another Person, one of his descendants, who would be a blessing for all the people of the world.

Abraham was looking first for a son, then for a nation which would come from his own bloodline. From those people One was to come to be that blessing – and that One is Jesus. In that sense Abraham was a stranger even in the land that God had promised him. Christians today should also consider that our lives on this earth are temporary; we are just traveling through. All who hope in Christ Jesus, then, need to remember that promise He made.

John 14:1 – 3

1 "Do not let your hearts be troubled.
You believe in God; believe also in me.

2 My Father's house has many rooms;
if that were not so, would I have told you
that I am going there to prepare a place for you?

3 And if I go and prepare a place for you,
I will come back and take you to be with me
that you also may be where I am.

The bodies we live in will not live forever, but Jesus is preparing a place for all who put their trust in God. Perhaps that is what Abraham had a glimpse of 4000 years ago! That is what the writer of Hebrews seems to say. In that foreign country,

he lived in tents, as did Isaac and Jacob,
who were heirs with him of the same promise.

10 For he was looking forward to
the city with foundations,
whose architect and builder is God (Hebrews 11:9b – 10).

There is much to learn from Abraham. He kept his vision, he kept his purpose, he kept his heart focused on God's promise.

Other passages have a significant relationship to this passage in Hebrews 11. They are: Revelation 21:6 – 8, 22:14 – 15; and Ephesians 2:14 – 16. The challenge of these three passages is another good reason for people everywhere to follow the example of Abraham. We must **keep our eyes fixed on Jesus, His teachings, and His personal examples while we live on this earth.** Through Jesus, God desires to bring peace to all people, but every one, individually, must want that peace **on God's terms, not ours.** Let Paul explain God's plan to bring peace to all mankind.

Ephesians 2:14 – 16

14 For he himself is our peace, who
has made the two groups one
and has destroyed the barrier, the
dividing wall of hostility,

15 by setting aside in his flesh the
law with its commands and

regulations. His purpose was to
create in himself one new
humanity out of the two, thus making peace,

16 and in one body to reconcile both
of them to God through
the cross, by which he put to death their hostility.

God did not intend for people to be divided for any reason – language, culture, race, skin color, or human tradition. Jesus came to unite all people, **Jew and Gentile**, into one new being in which God lives by His Spirit. The message of the two passages in Revelation is that our choice of behavior will determine our destiny. The New Jerusalem described in Revelation 21 is not to return to or rebuild the physical city of Jerusalem, because all the heavens and earth that we know of now will pass away. What Jesus is preparing for His people will be entirely new. (For more details on the final end of the heavens and the earth as we know them, read Revelation 21:7 – 15; and 2 Peter 3:8 – 18.)

Now, let John tell us what the angel guided him to write about the final separation. Our own personal choices in the war between good and evil will determine which way we will go. Will we decide to keep the faith, to keep on trusting God and His Truth, or will we choose to abandon that pathway to life and return deliberately to the ways of the world?

Revelation 21:6 – 8

6 He said to me: "It is done. I am
the Alpha and the Omega,
the Beginning and the End. To the thirsty I will give water
without cost from the spring of the water of life.

7 Those who are victorious will inherit all this,
and I will be their God and they will be my children.

8 But the cowardly, the unbelieving,
the vile, the murderers,
the sexually immoral, those who practice magic arts,
the idolaters and all liars—they will be consigned
to the fiery lake of burning sulfur.
This is the second death."

Revelation 22:14 – 15

14 "Blessed are those who wash
their robes, that they may
have the right to the tree of life and may go
through the gates into the city.

15 Outside are the dogs, those who practice magic arts,
the sexually immoral, the murderers, the idolaters
and everyone who loves and practices falsehood."

There will be a division in the last day and it will be based on what we, as individuals, choose to do in life. Do we choose to listen to God and seek His *water of life*, or choose to do what we please and suffer the eternal consequences? The second book in this **Trilogy of Clouds** will deal with the dark clouds described in these and many other warning passages in God's Word.

o o o o o

Bailiff: *Please present the evidence for*

The Faith of Abraham and Sarah

Me: *Thank you. Let us begin by examining*

Hebrews 11:11 – 12

*11 And by faith even Sarah, who
was past childbearing age,
was enabled to bear children because she
considered him faithful who had made the promise.*

*12 And so from this one man, and he as good as dead,
came descendants as numerous as the stars in the sky
and as countless as the sand on the seashore.*

Abraham is not the only one who maintained his faith in God for twenty-five years; Sarah waited that same twenty-five years for a son to be born. At one point, her faith must have weakened somewhat, and she thought she would help God by finding a surrogate mother for Abraham's son. And chaos was the result. Overall, however, she trusted that *God would be faithful to the promise He had made to Abraham twenty-five years before!* Both Abraham and Sarah were patient with God, and to spread that patience over twenty-five years is nothing short of amazing. How is our patience with God measured: in minutes? hours? days? Sarah and Abraham did not give up hope, and they were rewarded when God fulfilled that promise. We have much to learn about being patient in life, and especially with God.

Another event in the life of Abraham continues to stir the hearts of people today. God kept His promise to Abraham and Sarah and Isaac was born. When Isaac was a teenager, however, God gave a command to Abraham that must have struck deep into his heart. We should be very grateful that God does not use that same method of testing people today. Our faith is often tested but never like what Abraham faced 4000 years ago.

CHAPTER TWO

The Faith of Abraham Severely Tested

Bailiff: *Please present the text to be considered.*

Genesis 22:1 – 14

1 Some time later God tested Abraham. He said to him, "Abraham!" "Here I am," he replied.

2 Then God said, "Take your son, your only son, whom you love— Isaac—and go to the region of Moriah. Sacrifice him there as a burnt offering on a mountain I will show you."

Can we picture the anguish in Abraham's heart as he prepared to carry out God's instructions? Surely he did not sleep much that night, and surely he did not tell the boy's mother. What did he do?

3 Early the next morning Abraham got up and loaded his donkey. He took with him two of his servants and his son Isaac.

21

When he had cut enough wood for the burnt offering,
he set out for the place God had told him about.

4 On the third day Abraham looked up
and saw the place in the distance.

5 He said to his servants, "Stay here with the donkey
while I and the boy go over there.
We will worship and then we will come back to you."

6 Abraham took the wood for the
burnt offering and placed it
on his son Isaac, and he himself
carried the fire and the knife.
As the two of them went on together,

7 Isaac spoke up and said to his father Abraham,
"Father?" "Yes, my son?" Abraham replied.
"The fire and wood are here," Isaac said,
"but where is the lamb for the burnt offering?"

8 Abraham answered, "God himself
will provide the lamb for the
burnt offering, my son." And the two
of them went on together.

9 When they reached the place God
had told him about, Abraham
built an altar there and arranged
the wood on it. He bound
his son Isaac and laid him on the
altar, on top of the wood.

10 Then he reached out his hand and took the knife
to slay his son. 11 But the angel of the LORD called out

to him from heaven, "Abraham!
Abraham!" "Here I am," he replied.

12 "Do not lay a hand on the boy,"
he said. "Do not do anything
to him. Now I know that you fear
God, because you have not
withheld from me your son, your only son."

13 Abraham looked up and there in a
thicket he saw a ram caught
by its horns. He went over and took
the ram and sacrificed it
as a burnt offering instead of his son.

14 So Abraham called that place The LORD Will Provide.
And to this day it is said,
"On the mountain of the LORD it will be provided."

There is no record anywhere in the Scriptures of God ever testing the faith of any other person this way. God calls all Christians to become living sacrifices, not lambs to be slaughtered. Neither does He call for us to offer our own children as burnt offerings. Even though God allowed **His own Son, His unique Son,** to be nailed to a Roman cross, God does not punish people for their sins by demanding human sacrifice or crucifixion. No one can pay that price. God accepted the offering of Jesus; He paid the price for our sins. What does it mean to **become living sacrifices?** (Romans 12:1).

When we give up the old life of sin, and willingly allow Jesus to transform us into His image, we then become alive in Christ Jesus. Peter calls such believers *living stones* – to be built into a *spiritual house* (1 Peter 2:5). Paul calls it a *Holy temple in the Lord.* We are thus being built into a *dwelling in which God lives by His Spirit* (Ephesians 2:21 – 22). Jesus

23

continues to build this Holy temple, this dwelling in which we are to live because that is how God's Spirit lives in true believers.

Hebrews chapter 11 presents many examples of true witnesses of God. The writer calls them a **Great Cloud of Witnesses**, and that is what they are. Abraham himself lived a life of obedience to God, whether for commands to be carried out quickly, or a promise for which he had to wait many years. Abraham is a magnificent example of continuing to trust God for decades as he waited for God to fulfill His promise. Through Isaac, the descendants of Abraham became a great nation, as God had promised.

Of the four parts of the promise that God made to him, Abraham lived to see only two: to live in the land that was promised, and to realize that those around him respected his great name. Today, many call Abraham the father of the faithful. However, that exact expression is not found in the New Testament.

Romans 4:16 – 17

*16 Therefore, the promise comes by
faith, so that it may be by grace
and may be guaranteed to all Abraham's
offspring—not only to those
who are of the law but also to those
who have the faith of Abraham.
He is the father of us all.*

*17 As it is written: "I have made you a father
of many nations." He is our father in the sight of God,
in whom he believed—the God who gives life to the dead
and calls into being things that were not.*

Paul, in this letter to the Gentile Christians in Rome, states that the promise is for all who put their faith in God, whether as physical descendants of Abraham, or as Gentiles not under the law. In this way, Paul is saying, **He is the father of us all.** He repeats the idea in verse 17, **He** (Abraham) **is our father in the sight of God.** When our faith and trust in God are like that of Abraham, as faith begets faith, then Abraham is truly the father of the faithful. Let us understand that relationship in more detail.

There was no Jewish nation when Abraham was born, and none when he died. Of all the human beings on earth at that time, Abraham was the one who responded to God. The nation of Israel came long after God had changed the name of Abraham's grandson, Jacob, to Israel. Just as God had promised, the nation of Israel came into existence as the descendants of Abraham multiplied.

Ishmael, the son of Abraham and the slave, Hagar, was given a promise that a nation would also descend from him. God kept His promise to both of these sons. All of this concerns blood relationships, physical ties. How are Gentile Christians today the seed of Abraham? It is not by physical ties.

Our faith in God is the vital link to Abraham, whose example of faith is a brilliant light for all to see. When faith in God becomes strong like that of Abraham, we then have a spiritual connection to Abraham. Several passages help us understand this: Romans 3:21 – 31; Ephesians 2:11 – 22; 1 Peter 2:4 – 5; Colossians 3:1 – 17; and Galatians 3:26 – 29. The Galatians text gives a good summary of these passages.

Galatians 3:26 – 29

*26 So in Christ Jesus you are all
children of God through faith,*

*27 for all of you who were baptized into Christ
have clothed yourselves with Christ.*

*28 There is neither Jew nor Gentile,
neither slave nor free,*

*nor is there male and female, for you
are all one in Christ Jesus.*

*29 If you belong to Christ, then you are Abraham's seed,
and heirs according to the promise.*

Ephesians 2 reveals God's plan to bring peace to all the world, both Jew and Gentile, by the blood of the Lamb of God. Neither the bloodline connection of the Jewish people to Abraham, nor the "faith line" connection of the Gentiles to Abraham is able to bring us *into Christ Jesus.* Just as Abraham obeyed the call of God to come out of Ur, so must all people obey the call of God to come out of the slavery of sin, put all kinds of sin and evil to death. We are then to present our bodies, our minds, and our whole selves to Jesus allowing Him to make us into His image, *living stones in the Holy Temple of God.*

CHAPTER THREE

Evidence from Isaac, Jacob, Joseph, Parents of Moses, Moses, Children of Israel, Rahab, Gideon, Barak, Samson, Jephthah

Me: *Your Honor, the Hebrew writer lists Isaac,*
Jacob, and Joseph as part of the
Great Cloud of Witnesses,
but only mentions a few things about them.
May I present a Brief for each one with additional
Old Testament references for the
convenience of our readers?
Judge: *Yes, you may. Bailiff, continue*
to call the witnesses.

Bailiff: *Present your Brief for*

Isaac

Hebrews 11:20 refers to something that happened near the end of Isaac's life. Since the beginning of time, parents have experienced family upset caused by jealousy and sibling rivalry. The beginning of the problem between the twins, Esau and Jacob, is told in Genesis 25:24 – 34, when Esau sold his birthright to Jacob for a bowl of red stew. The background of this struggle involved both parents: Isaac, because he favored Esau, the hunter, who brought in the wild meats his father enjoyed eating; Rebekah, who favored Jacob, the gentler "home body." We must learn to avoid harmful family division. The resulting enmity between Jacob and Esau lasted many years before they found peace with each other (Genesis 33:1 – 15). However, Isaac blessed both of his sons before he died, but Jacob received the full birthright blessing (Genesis 27).

The story of Isaac finding a wife from among his own people is in Genesis 24. The very strong trust Abraham had in God was a great example for Isaac. Chapter 25 tells more of the events at the end of Abraham's life, and then his death.

o o o o o

Bailiff: Present your Brief for

Jacob

The life of Jacob is a very long story that not only completes the story of Esau and Jacob, it also intertwines with the next witness, Joseph. The whole story begins in Genesis 24:1 and continues to the end of Genesis at 50:26. In a strange way a family weakness can recur in succeeding generations, Jacob repeated his parents' mistake. We will learn more of this problem when we study the next witness from Hebrews 11.

When Esau was still angry and threatening to kill his twin, Rebekah learned about his threat. She talked with Jacob and told him to go to Haran and stay with her brother, Laban, until Esau calmed down. She then told Isaac that she did not want Jacob to marry a Canaanite woman, persuading Isaac to send Jacob to her brother's home, avoiding a tragedy. He was also charged to find a wife from among his mother's family. As

Jacob came near to Haran, he stopped at a well, and there met one of the daughters of Laban, and helped her draw water for her sheep.

After only one month with the family, Jacob had fallen in love with the beautiful shepherdess, Rachel, and wanted to marry her. Laban agreed to the marriage, but required Jacob to first work for him seven years. At the end of seven years, Laban, by devious means, gave Leah, the older sister, in marriage to Jacob. After the wedding night, Jacob realized the deception and called for a reckoning. Laban probably realized that Jacob had every right to be very angry. He then permitted Rachel to become Jacob's wife after Leah's bridal week was finished. However, he also required another seven years of work from Jacob.

The trust displayed in this series of events reveals some interesting information. Isaac did not want Jacob to marry a wife who came from a pagan society, so he sent him to Haran where he had blood ties. Thus the faith of Isaac is passed on to Jacob. We can observe this as he carried out his father's will, basically God's will, and found a wife he could be happy with. The story demonstrates the faith of Jacob, whose name God changed to Israel. This also shows a way to avoid and rectify mistakes in our own lives.

o o o o o

Bailiff: *Present your Brief for*

Joseph

At the close of his life Joseph still urged the people to remember the yet-to-come salvation from Egyptian slavery (Hebrews 11:22). There are many important events in Joseph's life: the death of his mother when his younger brother, Benjamin, was born; the acts of favoritism Jacob showered on Joseph with the resulting jealousy. His older brothers wanted to kill him, but finally decided to sell him as a slave to a band of Ishmaelite merchants, who were on their way to Egypt. There they sold him to Potiphar, captain of Pharaoh's guard (Genesis 35 – 37).

God was with Joseph in all his trials in Egypt, and reading the full account several times helps us to see just how closely God led, and how faithfully Joseph followed. There was another reconciliation in this family: Joseph and his brothers.

Joseph lived his adult life in complete trust in God. After Potiphar put him in prison, the warden recognized special qualities in Joseph (Genesis 39:20b – 23). Joseph interpreted dreams, stating clearly that the interpretations belonged to God (40:1 – 27). The same God-given qualities in Joseph were obvious when he interpreted Pharaoh's dreams (41:1 – 32). Faith and confidence in God were deep in the heart of Joseph as these events reveal. For our own faith to grow, we need to think about this amazing story often. Joseph was truly a part of that **Great Cloud of Witnesses.**

What a blessing to know this story and many other faith building accounts. Share these with your family. God's clear intention all along has been for believers to share sincere faith and God's truth with others. We must begin with our own young children, then reach out to other family members and friends. If we keep God's truth to ourselves, our faith will wane *and just might die.* What a tragedy that would be!

o o o o o

Bailiff: *Please present your evidence for*

The Parents of Moses

Generations after the death of Joseph, an edict of the king of Egypt was given to the Hebrew midwives: all the new-born male Hebrew children should be killed, but female infants were to be spared. However, the midwives *feared God more than they feared the edict of the king* (Exodus 1:15 – 22). The parents of Moses also feared God more than they feared the edict of the king, and found a way to keep their son, Moses, alive (Hebrews 11:23). Amram and Jochebed are listed as parents of Aaron, Moses, and Miriam (the oldest) in the genealogy of Levi (Numbers 26:59).

God allowed Moses to be brought up as the son of the king's daughter and be trained in all the wisdom of Egypt. Believing is important, but continuing to believe when faced with a threat of death is the proving ground of faith. The parents of Moses had that kind of courageous faith. They made a plan, carried it out, and saved the life of Moses.

Moses' mother made a basket of papyrus and put her baby in it. As her daughter watched, Jochebed launched the basket into the Nile river. Pharaoh's daughter saw the basket and ordered her slave girl to get it. She found a crying infant inside, had compassion, and took the child to be her own. When Miriam saw that Pharaoh's daughter wanted the child, she approached and asked if she needed a Hebrew nurse to care for the child. The princess agreed – and whom should this sister get? Moses' own mother, of course! (Exodus 2:1 – 10).

Moses lived in Pharaoh's house for forty years, learning all the ways of the Egyptians. However, Jochebed evidently had taught Moses who he was, and who his people were, greatly influencing his heart. Did she teach him because of her own natural, motherly desire to nurture her son, or was God guiding her actions? However it was, what followed has the imprint of God's will throughout.

o o o o o

Bailiff: *Please present your evidence for*

Moses, to whom God gave the Ten Commandments

*24 By faith Moses, when he had grown
up, refused to be known
as the son of Pharaoh's daughter.*

*25 He chose to be mistreated along
with the people of God
rather than to enjoy the fleeting pleasures of sin.*

The Old Covenant books of Exodus, Leviticus, Numbers, and Deuteronomy tell how God used Moses to accomplish His will. The faith that Moses had in God can be seen throughout these four books. We know Moses had complete trust in God because of his obedience.

There were three forty-year periods in Moses' life. In the first we learn that he was trained in all the wisdom of Egypt. This may seem contrary to developing his faith in God. But remember that God was involved in all that took place during that period. Remember also that it was his own mother who nursed Moses, and cared for him on behalf of Pharaoh's daughter. What did his mother do during all those years, however many there were? She taught him who he was, a descendant of Abraham, Isaac, and Jacob, an Israelite! (Exodus 2:1 – 10).

That is why he reacted so violently and killed the Egyptian who was abusing a Hebrew. Moses thought no one had seen this, but someone knew (Exodus 2:11 – 14). As a result, he fled from the anger of Pharaoh and went far away from Egypt.

He spent the second forty-year period in Midian where he married Zipporah, who bore him two sons (Exodus 2:15 – 22, 18:1 – 4). Toward the end of that period Moses had an encounter with God, which would send him back to Egypt to begin the last forty year period.

The voice that came from a bush that was burning, *but not being consumed*, convinced Moses that he was standing on holy ground. **Moses knew that God had been talking to him!** Even though he argued with God before finally agreeing to obey, he knew that he was to follow whatever God told him to do.

God commanded Moses to bring the Israelites out of slavery in Egypt back to the land promised to Abraham and his descendants. After many troubles in Egypt, and after God performed many wonders through Moses and Aaron, and after the death of all the firstborn in Egypt, Pharaoh finally agreed to let the Hebrews leave Egypt. However, leading over two million people through the Red Sea and through rough, wilderness territory for forty years was a severe challenge to the leadership of Moses, and to his faith in God.

The people complained to Moses because there was not enough water for the people and their livestock. They also complained because they missed the food they had enjoyed in Egypt. Moses and Aaron then went to the tabernacle and fell face down into the presence of God, who gave them instructions. God told them to call the people together and in their presence *speak to a rock,* which would then pour out water, enough for all the people and their livestock! The full account is in Numbers 20:2 – 12.

Moses was positive that water would come out of that rock! He had no doubt whatsoever. Perhaps we do not have that kind of knowledgeable faith, but by watching how Moses obeyed, we see an outstanding trust. That is something for us to aim for. But sometimes leaders make big mistakes, and Moses was no exception.

It is easy to understand why Moses was exasperated with these non-trusting, complaining people, why he called them rebels. "*Listen, you rebels, must we bring you water out of this rock?*" They *were* rebels, but Moses created two problems for himself. It is not only what Moses said, *must we bring you water,* but also what he did: *Then Moses raised his arm and struck the rock twice with his staff.* When Moses said, *must we,* he placed himself on the same level as God. In his anger over the grumbling of the Hebrews, he allowed the ugly head of arrogance to control what he did. When he struck the rock with his staff, which God had commanded on an earlier occasion (Exodus 17:3 – 6), his exasperation with the complaining people caused him to overrule what God had just told him to do – *speak to the rock* (Numbers 20:9).

The result of Moses' disobedience should be a warning for leaders today. Some seem to think they have the power and authority of God over people. The words of Jesus from Matthew 4:4 come to mind again: *"It is written: 'Man shall not live on bread alone, but on every word that comes from the mouth of God.'"* Jesus is quoting from Deuteronomy 8:3, which means that this principle, paying close attention to *every word that comes from the mouth of God,* has been, is now, and will always be what God expects of all of us.

Because of his disobedience, Moses was not allowed to take the children of Israel into the promised land. He was permitted only to look across the Jordan River. We can learn steadfast faith from Moses, and we can also learn much from his disobedience. We can learn to *keep our eyes fixed on Jesus* and not run ahead. We can learn that we are servants of the Lord, not rule makers or judges. And, we can all learn that when the Lord God of the universe gives directions, He does not waste words. Therefore, we need to give heed to *every word that proceeds from the mouth of God.*

o o o o o

Bailiff: *Please present your evidence for*

The Children of Israel

Selections from Exodus 16:1 – 36

How much faith did these two million descendants of Abraham have when they followed Moses? The Egyptian chariots were rapidly approaching to attack and take them back into slavery, and the Red Sea was blocking any escape. Moses, by his great trust in God, took his shepherd's staff and led them down the banks of the Red Sea to cross over safely!

We can see clearly both the faith of Moses and the faith of the people of Israel as they hurried to the other side of the Red Sea. Not one person stayed on the bank *verbalizing* his faith; every one of them, men, women, and children, had the kind of active faith that pleases God: they trustingly followed God's chosen leader, Moses.

Later, when the people wavered and wanted to go back to Egypt, Moses kept them headed for the promised land. When they could not find water, Moses **cried out to the Lord** (Exodus 15:25). When the people complained about the lack of good food, God heard their grumbling and told Moses and Aaron what to do (Exodus 15:22 – 16:36). The people had a hard time doing the exact things God told them to do. (What about the people of today; is it any easier for us?) God gave them the quail and manna *for forty years!* (Joshua 5:10 – 12).

Because of their unfaithfulness, most of the Israelites who had left Egypt with Moses died before reaching Canaan (Numbers 14:20 – 38). The only people God allowed to enter the promised land were Joshua and Caleb, and those who had been twenty years of age or under when they escaped from their bondage in Egypt. Even Moses was not allowed to cross the Jordan River; he could only look over into the Promised Land from the eastern side (Deuteronomy 32:44 – 52).

Joshua became the strong, faithful, and courageous servant of God to lead the people across the Jordan River to Jericho. (Note: The account of the capture of Jericho is not listed as a witness in Hebrews 11, but is included with the witness of the Children of Israel.) The soldiers marched around that walled city once a day for six days, and then seven times on the seventh day. Did the soldiers realize how much fear was generated in the hearts of the people inside those walls (Joshua 5:13 – 6:27).

What we are seeing here is a chain of faith: God told Joshua what to have the soldiers do; he trusted God and ordered the soldiers to do it. Then the soldiers had to trust the commands of Joshua and the soldiers' trust came from the trust Joshua had in God. Are we not to set an example of complete trust in God in the presence of our children so that they can learn and follow? And, should we not exhibit that same kind of trust in the presence of all the people we meet?

The pattern of behavior of the Israelites during their time in the wilderness is similar to the pattern described throughout the book of Judges: forget God, suffer, beg forgiveness, return to God; forget again, suffer again, beg God again, return to God for a short time. The problem: **They did not listen to God and did what was right in their own eyes** (Judges 17:6; 21:25).

Thinking about all this can help us analyze the pattern of our own behavior and determine to listen more closely to all of God's words. We need to think deeply about every word that Jesus said, and each example He set, to draw us back to God and His love. We need to realize that every word spoken by Jesus is for our good. God is love. God is good. God is merciful. God is forgiving. But God also expects us to both learn and practice the same kind of love, goodness, mercy, and forgiveness. May God help all of us *to keep our eyes fixed on Jesus!*

Me: *Even the writer of the Hebrew letter*
stated that he did not have time
to tell all the stories concerning this Great
Cloud of Witnesses (Hebrews 11:32).
I will therefore present briefs as needed as we did earlier.
Judge: *Bailiff, please call for each brief in order.*

Bailiff: *Present your Brief for*

Rahab

God expects us to put our trust in His words and teachings. In this case, the trust required was based on an agreement between Rahab and the two spies Joshua had sent into Jericho. She hid them from her own people and arranged for them to escape. Rahab, as anyone might have done, bargained for the lives of all her family. The two spies also needed some protection since they were only two against the whole army of Jericho. The agreement between the spies and Rahab is recorded in Joshua 2, and we read how the agreement was honored in Joshua 6:17b. The continued safety for all of her family is recorded in 6:25.

A strong trust relationship between a human being and God is magnificent; trust relationships between people must be based on the eternal principles of God's truth.

o o o o o

Bailiff: *Present your Brief for*

Gideon

During the period of the Judges, the Jewish people frequently forgot the God who had saved them from slavery in Egypt. They began to worship the idols of the people who lived around them. If people forget the God of salvation and love, and engage in idol worship, the result is trouble, wherever it happens. Without God's protection, the enemy has a free reign to do whatever he wishes. Gideon lived when the Jewish people had to hide in caves, or in remote mountain places, to escape these enemies that lived all around them. His account is recorded in three chapters of Judges: 6, 7, and 8.

It is no wonder that Gideon responded as he did when the angel of the Lord called him with these words, **The Lord is with you, mighty warrior.** Gideon was not sure this angel was talking to the right person; he really wondered if the Lord could be with the Israelites when *the strong Midianite army was in full control!* The exchange between Gideon and the angel of the Lord is related in Judges 6:14 – 16.

The Lord told Gideon that He was sending him in strength to save Israel from the hand of Midian, but Gideon had questions and excuses. *How can I save Israel? I am from the smallest tribe and I am the smallest in my family.* The Lord assured him that He was with him and that he would prevail over Midian completely.

Gideon has been criticized for asking for so many assurances, and questioning why the angel was talking to him, rather than to someone more "qualified." It took a while for Gideon to understand that God **was calling him**. When Gideon accepted that God had called him to lead this dangerous task, he did not flinch.

Later, God put Gideon to the test. Rather than send the 32,000 soldiers into this battle, God told Gideon to send the fearful home; 22,000 men left. Then God told Gideon that there were still too many men; God narrowed the number to 300! That is when Gideon asked for proof that this was God giving the command. God gave him the proof. Let each of us ask, *Would my faith be as strong?*

With the continued help of God, Gideon carried out his mission completely, placing an amazing amount of trust in God who gave the orders. That is why Gideon is a part of that *Great Cloud of Witnesses.*

How did 300 men put to rout the whole Midianite army? One dark night, each of Gideon's men was given a trumpet and a lighted torch hidden in a big jar. They were divided into three companies and stealthily surrounded the sleeping camp. Just as the encamped soldiers were changing the mid-watch, Gideon gave the signal. The sound of 300 crashing jars exposing 300 torches and the simultaneous blast of 300 trumpets caused the suddenly awakened soldiers to believe they were surrounded by a large army. They saw people moving about within their camp, mistaking them for the enemy. In their confusion, the Midianites began to kill each other.

Fear and confusion brought on the defeat of the whole Midianite army. It was Gideon's trust in God's plan that won the victory.

o o o o o

Bailiff: *Present your Brief for*

Barak

Typical behavior of the Israelites during the period of the Judges again found the Israelites bowing down to senseless idols. They had been under the control of Eglon, King of Moab, for eighteen years, when they again cried to the Lord for relief. God raised up Ehud to conquer the king of Moab, and it brought peace to Israel for forty years (Judges 3:12 – 30).

But after the death of Ehud, the people again did evil in the sight of the Lord. For this evil, God allowed Jabin, a king in Canaan, to make trouble. He gave Sisera, a commander of 900 iron chariots, the authority to mercilessly persecute the Israelites for twenty years. After suffering for so long, they again cried to the Lord for help (4:3).

People make mistakes, and Barak, a military leader of 10,000 men, and listed in the **Great Cloud of Witnesses** (Hebrews 11:32), made one big mistake. When Deborah, a prophetess and judge of Israel at that time, relayed God's command to Barak to fight Sisera, he did not immediately obey.

Barak was not exactly bargaining with the Lord for he did not say, *Dear Lord, if you will do this for me, I will lead the army to destroy Sisera and his 900 chariots of iron.* Barak knew God was commanding him to go and fight Sisera. But without asking God's permission, Barak said he would not go, that is, not carry out the command of God, unless Deborah went with him. *Barak made his obedience conditional.*

What was Barak thinking? Why did he make such a condition? Only God knows what was in Barak's mind, but it was a terrible mistake. He was saying, in effect, that if Deborah did not go with him he *would not obey a command from God!* It may disturb us to think of our making the same kind of mistake because it seems so strange. In spite of his mistake, we must not miss the deep down faith of Barak: God sent him a message through Deborah; he believed it and eventually carried out the command. His faith in God is a great example, but how can we avoid making a similar mistake?

o o o o o

Bailiff: *Present your Brief for*

Samson

The story of Samson is found in four chapters of Judges: 13 – 16. As children in Bible class, we remember Samson as a strong hero who tore a lion apart, pulled the city gates down and carried them to the top of a hill, but we do not remember anyone ever **emphasizing God's purpose** in all this. God had a plan for Samson *before he was even conceived in his mother's womb!* (Judges 13:1 – 5). The Israelites brought problems on themselves when they quit trusting God and His guidance. They worshiped the local idols and walked in evil paths. But God still cared for His people.

However, they had to repent and come back to God. The Israelites had the freedom to choose to trust God or not. As mentioned before, their history was a cycle: trusting God, not trusting God, suffering the consequences, begging God to overthrow their oppressors, trusting again, but soon falling away again . . . time after time after time! God brought Samson into this world to take vengeance on the oppressors; that was his task.

Samson *was* an answer to the prayers of a childless couple. An angel foretold what would happen, and explained the conditions established by God. Samson knew that his strength was given to him by God for the purpose of relieving the oppression of the Philistines, and other enemies. By human weakness, Samson stumbled in his trust in God, and he lost his amazing strength. When he entrusted the secret of his strength to Delilah, she had his hair shaved off, then betrayed him to the Philistines. His eyes were gouged out, and he was put in prison to work much like an animal, grinding grain in the prison. When his faith re-awakened and his strength returned, God gave Sampson the opportunity to accomplish in his death what he had been sent to do! (Judges 16:1 – 31).

The witness of Samson may be stated simply: during the time of his greatest suffering, he did not ask God to relieve his suffering, but rather to allow him to complete his God-given task. **That is the kind of faith that Samson had!** Read these four chapters again, **remembering that God had** raised up Samson to avenge the oppression of His people.

**Me: *Your Honor, we need to present both the faith of Jephthah and the tragic part of his life in more detail.*
Judge: *I concur. Bailiff, call the prophet.***

Bailiff: *Please present the evidence for*

Jephthah

When Israel forgot the God who loved them, and again worshiped the idols of the people among whom they lived, they suffered. They suffered greatly, sometimes for many years. When their suffering became unbearable, they would again beg God to save them. But this time they tried the very patience of God. He said this to them.

14 "Go and cry out to the gods you have chosen.
Let them save you when you are in trouble!"

The Israelites then knew that they had sinned grossly; this was their reply.

15 . . . "We have sinned. Do with us
whatever you think best,
but please rescue us now."

Their reply was followed by action.

16 Then they got rid of the foreign gods among them
and served the Lord . . .

The last part of this same verse reveals God's true heart of love.

And he could bear Israel's misery no longer.

Remember, God did not allow Abraham to sacrifice Isaac as a burnt offering. At no other time did God command human sacrifice, except when Jesus offered Himself for all people. But just as God *could bear Israel's misery no longer,* we see the love of God taking control.

That *Great Cloud of Witnesses* reveals many aspects of the Creator of the universe, the Creator of all life, the Identifier of all that is good. Just before Jephthah comes on the scene, we see just how bad things were for the descendants of Abraham – because they had turned away from God, bowed down to sensual idols, and worshiped the many gods of the people among whom they lived (Judges 10:6 – 18). Jephthah's part is recorded in 11:1 – 12:7.

There is no record **in this account** of the Israelites offering their own children to these man-made gods during the three hundred years of the Judges. Later, however, the Israelites did offer their own children as burnt sacrifices to the same idols. (See 2 Chronicles 28:3, 33:6; Jeremiah 7:31, 19:5, 32:34 – 35; Ezekiel 20:31, 23:37 – 39.) Now, who is this Jephthah and how does human sacrifice enter the picture?

Gilead and his wife had many sons. Jephthah was also Gilead's son, but his mother was a prostitute. When these sons had grown up, the blood-brothers drove Jephthah away, not willing for him to share in the family inheritance. Jephthah, a skilled warrior, fled to Tob where he found others who recognized his leadership (11:1 – 3).

Trouble again came to the Israelites and the elders of Gilead went to Tob to beg Jephthah to be their leader. They needed a military leader to fight the approaching Ammonite army. We learn of Jephthah's faith in God from the answer he gave those elders. He asked a question. "*Suppose you take me back to fight the Ammonites and the Lord gives them to me – will I really be your head?*" (11:9). If there was to be a victory, Jephthah knew that it would be because God would be with him.

God chose Jephthah, a cast out half-brother, because He knew Jephthah would look to Him for guidance. This demonstrates another attribute of God, found throughout the Old and New Testaments. God sometimes chooses an unlikely person to carry out a task. A classic example is Saul, an enemy and persecutor of Christians. Jesus chose him to become an apostle to proclaim the Gospel to the Gentiles.

Jephthah went with the elders of Israel and they did make him the ruler over all the people. We see his faith in God as he *repeated all his words before the Lord in Mizpah* (11:11). He began his rule by communicating with the King of Ammon. Jephthah had a clear understanding of the history of his people, and explained that the King of Ammon did not have a legitimate

43

claim to the land occupied by the Israelites (11:14 – 27). The king paid no attention to the message of Jephthah (11:28). As Jephthah advanced to conquer the Ammonites, he made a vow to the Lord.

Judges 11:30 – 31, 35

30 . . . "If you give the Ammonites into my hands,

31 whatever comes out of the door
of my house to meet me
when I return in triumph from the
Ammonites will be the LORD's,
and I will sacrifice it as a burnt offering."

The Lord God of Heaven and Earth gave Jephthah the victory, and Israel subdued Ammon. But for Jephthah, the joys of victory did not last long.

Jephthah returned home to Mizpah, a victorious leader of Israel. Who should come out of the door of his house to greet him with dancing to the tambourines but his daughter, *his only child!* Jephthah had made a vow to God. This vow was made without thinking of the possible consequences. It was not needed because God's Spirit had already been given to Jephthah (11:29). He cried out to his daughter.

35 . . . "Oh no, my daughter!
You have brought me down and I am devastated.
I have made a vow to the Lord that I cannot break."

His daughter realized the seriousness of her father's vow to God – it must not be broken. She submitted to her father, but asked for two months with her friends before returning for her father to keep his burnt-offering vow to God (11:36 – 39).

44

There are two lessons for all believers: t
Jephthah's faith in God, and the danger of m
God. Jephthah trusted God and God had al'
His Spirit. His faith was obviously very stro'
try to judge Jephthah for making the vow, but w...
the terrible consequences of his vow, we must reconsider this
situation. One vow made to God in haste led to the death of his
own daughter, and it brought on a lifetime of regret, remorse,
and bewilderment for what he had done.

CHAPTER FOUR

Samuel: Judge, Prophet, and Priest of God

Bailiff: *Please present your evidence for*

An Unusual Beginning

Elkanah had two wives, Peninnah and Hannah. Peninnah had children but Hannah was barren. Peninnah made fun of Hannah because she had no sons to give to Elkanah. Every year Elkanah took both wives to Shiloh to offer sacrifices in the temple of the Lord, where Eli and his two sons were serving as priests.

One day, after making the sacrifices at the temple, Hannah stood up and began to pray silently, her lips moving, but no sound coming from her mouth. When Eli saw her, he accused her of being drunk. Hannah told him emphatically that she was not drunk, but that she **was pouring out her soul to the Lord** (1 Samuel 1:15). Eli sent her away in peace and said, **"May the God of Israel grant you what you have asked of Him."** God did bless Hannah with a son and she named him Samuel.

Hannah determined for Samuel to serve the Lord and planned, after weaning him, to take him to Eli to be raised in the temple of the Lord and serve God all his life. After this, Hannah had three other sons and two daughters. Hannah made priestly

47

clothes for Samuel each year while he was growing up and took them to him. Even as a child, Samuel wore the garments of a priest, but how do we know that God also had chosen Samuel? The scripture states that he **grew up in the presence of the Lord** (1 Samuel 2:21b).

The innocence of a young lad is seen in what took place one night as both Eli and Samuel were sleeping. Samuel heard his name called, got up and went into Eli's room and said, **Here am I, you called me.** It was only after the third time this happened that Eli realized it was the Lord who was calling Samuel (1 Samuel 3:8 – 18).

Eli told Samuel to go back to bed, then told him how to answer if the Lord called him again by saying, **Speak, LORD, for your servant is listening.** When Samuel heard his name called again, that is the way he answered. Samuel listened as God told him what He planned to do to Eli and his descendants. His sons had blasphemed God and Eli did not restrain them. The young Samuel was rightly disturbed.

The next morning, Samuel got up and opened the doors, evidently one of his regular chores, but he was afraid to tell Eli about the vision he had seen the night before. However, Eli knew that God had told Samuel something and he pressured the boy to tell everything. Samuel did not hide anything from the old priest. Eli's response revealed that he had to *just leave it in God's hand*s, there was no more he could do. He simply said, **He is the LORD; let him do what is good in his eyes** (3:18).

God had called Samuel into His very serious service. The sons of Eli, who were serving as priests, had done many evil things. They had contempt for the sacrifices made by the people. God reprimanded Eli **because he did not restrain his sons**. God told Samuel that He planned to remove Eli and his sons from the priesthood. This kept all of his descendants from ever serving as priests (1 Samuel 3:1 – 14).

The demonstration of Samuel's faith in God can be seen in the many ways he served God. He was the last of the judges, served as a priest, and was recognized as a prophet of the Lord. His constant dependence on God's message for his actions sets a standard that is difficult for us to follow. Samuel lived it day by day while some of us seem to live it only on Sunday. Let us humbly learn from this great witness.

Samuel Recognized as a Prophet, Leader, and Judge

The term, *from Dan to Beersheba (*Dan in the north and Beersheba in the south), included all the people of Israel; they all recognized Samuel as a prophet (1 Samuel 3:19 – 21). It is also stated that Samuel was a leader of Israel as long as he lived. He went to these towns to serve as judge: Bethel, Gilgal, Mizpah, and Ramah, his home. He built an altar to God in his home town (7:15 – 17).

The Faith of Samuel to Be Our Example

The writers of the Bible sometimes narrate a broad overview of an event, then follow it with more details, usually in chronological order. The whole life of Samuel was dedicated to God, listening to His words, and telling the people of Israel what God expected of them. Our main purpose is to see the faith of these **Clouds of Witnesses** and absorb the power of God-pleasing faith.

When Samuel had grown old, he appointed two of his sons to be judges in Israel. However, they did not walk in the ways that God had shown Samuel. This disturbed the elders of Israel and they came together to talk to Samuel about this matter. They did not ask Samuel to appoint someone else to be judges; they just asked Samuel to give them a king. Can we imagine how Samuel reacted to this? He took it as a personal rejection of his own leadership.

Samuel immediately turned to God in prayer. From God's response to Samuel's prayer, we learn that God knew Samuel felt rejected by the people. God answered his prayer and reassured Samuel in several ways. God told him that what the people were saying to him was not a rejection of him or his leadership, but it was a rejection of God as king. God reminded Samuel that the people had been rejecting Him since they left Egypt, and had returned to their worship of idols. Samuel was again told to *listen to them,* but he was also to warn them what a king would claim as his "rights" over them.

When Samuel felt troubled, he did not try to hide anything from God. He humbly sought the guidance of God, and this seeking came from the very heart of Samuel. What were the people really asking for? Why did they want a king? God told Samuel to warn the people about the troubles they would have under a king. Even though Samuel spoke kindly to them, their response was very disappointing.

They would not listen to Samuel or acknowledge the warnings, but insisted, *We want a king to rule over us, then we can be like all the nations around us.* However, there is one more thing about what they wanted that reveals so much of human nature. *They wanted a king that would fight their battles for them* (1 Samuel 8:19 – 20).

Samuel was very much disappointed when the elders continued to beg for a king. Even after he had warned them about the troubles that would result from this change of leadership, they still insisted on having their own way. God gave them *what they were asking for.*

Samuel's obedient trust in God did not waver; he carried out God's command and anointed their new king. The Israelite people suffered many years because they had failed to offer sincere prayers for *God's will to be done.* Do we ask for things we want without thinking of the long-range consequences? Or are we like these Jewish elders and just want to be "like the nations around us"?

There are three things we should think about. One, Samuel did not hesitate to obey the instructions of God. Two, God allowed the people the freedom of choice. (Samuel knew they were making the wrong decision, but he carried out the instructions just as God had given him.) Three, the Israelites blindly disregarded the warnings God had given them through Samuel.

Their arguing point: **then we will be like all the other nations, with a king to lead us and to go out before us and fight our battles** (8:20). They closed their ears to the warnings, and much trouble came upon them!

Do we have a strong desire to do what everyone else is doing and wear the latest fashions "everybody else" is wearing? Are we looking for someone else to fight our battles so that we can "do our own thing"? The wrong decision of the Israelite leaders brought dire consequences, and so will *our* wrong decisions. Can someone else really fight our battles for us? We must all fight *individually* against the evils in this world. Let us face the truth: **there are very serious consequences for every bad decision.**

Two events intersect with Samuel, the prophet, and Saul, a future king. First, Saul and a servant were out looking for his father's donkeys, could not find them, and Saul decided to return home. However, the servant suggested that they go find a respected prophet whose words always came true. Saul took the advice of his servant and they went to find this prophet (1 Samuel 9:1 – 10).

The second event that brought Samuel and Saul together came about this way. The day before they met, God had appeared to Samuel and told him that this Saul was His choice to lead Israel. On first meeting Saul, Samuel told him that the donkeys had been found, and invited both Saul and his servant to be special guests at his banquet. At the end of the dinner, Samuel called Saul aside and told him what God had revealed to him. After anointing Saul (1 Samuel 10:1), Samuel told him several things he would experience on his way home (10:2 – 5). He concluded his prophecy to Saul with the following amazing words.

1 Samuel 10:6 – 7

*6 The Spirit of the LORD will come powerfully upon you,
and you will prophesy with them;
and you will be changed into a different person.*

*7 Once these signs are fulfilled, do whatever your
hand finds to do, for God is with you.*

Saul returned home and began plowing his father's fields. When he learned how the Ammonites threatened the Israelites in Jabesh Gilead, the Spirit of God came upon Saul. He gathered a huge army, soundly defeating the Ammonites (11:11). After this great victory, some of the people called for those who opposed the kingship of Saul to be put to death. Saul denied their demands and gave God the glory for the victory.

1 Samuel 11:14

*No one shall be put to death today,
for this day the Lord has rescued Israel.*

Again, it was Samuel who called for Saul to be reaffirmed as king. It seemed to be easy for Samuel to carry out God's commands, even though he knew the people had not made a wise choice. But even after all this, the people still needed to be sure that Saul was to be their king. Several days prior to this, Samuel had given some very specific instructions to Saul.

1 Samuel 10:8

*"Go down ahead of me to Gilgal. I will surely come down
to you to sacrifice burnt offerings
and fellowship offerings,
but you must wait seven days until I come to you and
tell you what you are to do."*

Notice: *Go down ahead of me to Gilgal; you must wait seven days.* Saul understood the *"Go"* command, and the *"wait seven days"* command, but he did not pay attention to the last part, *"until I come to you and tell you what you are to do."* Even though God was with him, Saul still was expected to wait for instructions from God, through Samuel, before acting – *but he did not wait* (1 Samuel 13).

Saul made two huge mistakes: one, he thought he had the authority to offer the sacrifices and fellowship offerings; two, he did not wait for Samuel to arrive and tell him *what he should do.* How very important it is for all of us today to learn how to listen to every word of the Lord, to think deeply about the instructions He has given us. His words have come not only from the prophets, but also from Jesus and those He chose to fill with God's Holy Spirit and give the world a New Covenant.

Our purpose is to see this great cloud of prophets who foretold many events in the lives of the children of Israel. We realize that Saul failed to understand how to listen to God. God wants us to reason together and think about what He is saying to us. Problems come when we try to bend the will of God to conform to *what we think best.* Saul's example should be a warning, so that we will focus on God's whole message.

Another example of this kind of false reasoning is found in chapter 15, where Saul followed most – but not all – of the commands of God. He allowed his soldiers to bring back the best sheep and cattle, fat calves and lambs, everything that was good. He himself brought back King Agag. All this was contrary to God's instructions. Samuel confronted Saul with a strong rebuke by asking one serious question which he explained in detail.

1 Samuel 15:22 – 23

22 But Samuel replied:
"Does the LORD delight in burnt offerings and sacrifices

as much as in obeying the LORD?
To obey is better than sacrifice,
and to heed is better than the fat of rams.

23 For rebellion is like the sin of divination,
and arrogance like the evil of idolatry.
Because you have rejected the word of the LORD,
he has rejected you as king."

At Gilgal Saul did not realize the importance of waiting for additional instructions from God. In the war against the Amalekites, he did not realize the importance of keeping every detail of God's commands. In both cases, Saul was relying upon his own judgment rather than depending upon the guidance of God. Jesus made the importance of listening carefully to God very clear when He spoke to Satan.

Matthew 4:4

Man does not live on bread alone, but on every word that comes from the mouth of God.

Should not each of us ask – *Is my faith strong enough to sincerely look at every detail of God's word and see how it applies to me?* Perhaps we need to be much more aware of God's full message!

God gave Samuel the responsibility to tell Saul that he was being rejected as king, causing Samuel to be afraid of Saul. Remember, Saul was a big strong warrior and had already demonstrated that he could do things without thinking about the consequences. However, God had already chosen the next family from which to anoint a new king. He called Samuel to go to the house of Jesse.

Samuel was afraid that Saul, on hearing what Samuel's mission was, would try to kill him. But God gave him a way to escape. Samuel obeyed and went to the house of Jesse, trusting God to keep him safe (1 Samuel 16:1 – 13).

Do we in this present world, in order to keep the faith, sometimes have to walk into the face of danger? Now, all over the world, believers are called on to remain faithful, not only in the face of danger, but far too often in the face of death. May God help all of us, whatever we may face, to hold on to our faith, to keep our trust in God firm to the end! That is our hope, and why we need to give very serious, deep thought to God's every word *and let our faith grow strong!*

Samuel then confronted the people with questions which challenged them to face the reality of God's kingship. *Have I ever stolen anything from you? Accepted a bribe? Have I ever cheated any of you?* They answered with these words.

1 Samuel 12:4

You have not cheated or oppressed us, you have not taken anything from anyone's hand.

After that, Samuel called the people together to review what God had done for them, and what they, as a people, had done. Samuel reminded them of Moses and Aaron leading them out of the slavery of Egypt into the land of promise. Samuel also reminded them of how they had soon forgotten God's blessings. They began to worship the idols of the people around them. Their enemies caused them great suffering and they cried out to the Lord for help, confessing their sins.

This happened repeatedly during the period of the Judges. God sent leaders to rescue them, but they soon forgot and again regressed into sin and idolatry. It seems they could not learn. They went to Samuel and asked for a king. The most important thing they had forgotten was that *God was their King,* but in their stubbornness, they continued to want a king to *fight our battles for us.*

Samuel then told them He had given them the king they had asked for, but that God still expected them, **and their new king**, to serve and obey Him. Otherwise the hand of God would be against them. As a means of verifying that Samuel was the servant of God and the warning he was giving them was from God, he told them to watch what would happen.

As a twelve-year-old boy, Enoch had an experience in a wheat field. His task was to pick up the bundles of wheat dropped from the cutting and binding machine, and stack them, stalk ends on the ground. Several of these bound bundles were stacked together and a few bundles were placed on top in what was called a shock. Why was this important? If the grain ends were on the ground and rains came, the grain would rot quickly. During the wheat harvesting season, rain can be an enemy, especially if the grain has not been cut and stacked properly. So, Samuel asked about the season, **is it not wheat harvesting time?** Then he called to God and the rains came with the thunder. This means that there was some wind with it, and the ripe wheat, heavy on their stalks, became wet and bent to the ground – meaning that most, if not all of the crop, was lost.

Then the people realized that they had sinned against God, not only in asking for a king, but by worshiping idols **who could not rescue them.** Samuel told them to revere God and serve Him faithfully **with all your heart.** They needed to remember all the good things God had done for them for hundreds of years! Wow! What a challenge for us! Since the promise God made to Abraham, we have 4000 years of good things God has done for His people, good things for us to appreciate. The crowning gift, however, is **what Jesus did for us on the cross!**

Samuel sternly warned the people, **If you go back to doing evil, both you and your king will perish.** This warning also applies to us, regardless of what our "king" might be: money, power, lands, recognition, control, or whatever gets in the way of reverence for God and our faithful, *joyful service as His Children of Light.*

Samuel urged the people to be obediently faithful to God, all the time, and in all their ways. Somehow, in today's world, it seems of paramount importance for Christians to attend at least one Sunday worship service. Do that and you are "all OK" with God? An attitude like this puts God into our lives as a "good ole boy," rather than a God who can live in our hearts and help us become like Him, like Jesus. Is not this charge from Samuel to the Israelites also a strong message for us?

How strong was the faith of Samuel to deliver such a challenge, such an absolute charge to the people of Israel! Since the beginning of time, God has always expected people to make a choice between two extremes: Listen obediently to God and live; or turn away from God and die. Generations before, Joshua, another great leader, had also made a strong but clear challenge to the people of Israel.

Joshua 24:14 – 15

14 "Now fear the Lord and serve him with all faithfulness. Throw away the gods your ancestors worshiped beyond the Euphrates River and in Egypt, and serve the Lord.

15 But if serving the Lord seems undesirable to you, then choose for yourselves this day whom you will serve, whether the gods your ancestors served beyond the Euphrates, or the gods of the Amorites, in whose land you are living. But as for me and my household, we will serve the Lord"

It seems to me that neither Samuel nor Joshua was talking about a "Sunday-morning-only faith." Joshua had led the

Israelites into the land promised to them by God, but there were still idol worshipers all around them, people who did evil things in their devotion to false gods. Joshua told them they had to make a choice about whom they would serve *and that choice was their personal responsibility.* **God does not force anyone to accept His gracious gifts, but calls for us to choose, just like Joshua.**

> *. . . choose for yourselves this day*
> *whom you will serve . . .*

CHAPTER FIVE

David, From Brave Shepherd Lad to Valiant, God-trusting, King of all Israel

Bailiff: *Please present the evidence from* The Life of David, Son of Jesse

After He had told Samuel He was rejecting Saul as king, God sent Samuel to the home of an Israelite named Jesse. When Samuel looked at seven of his eight sons, he was pleased with their appearance. But God told him that none of them was His choice. So Samuel asked Jesse if he had any more sons. He replied that his youngest son was out tending the sheep. When David, the youngest, came before Samuel, God told him this was the one He had chosen (1 Samuel 16:1 – 13). God told Samuel to anoint David, and, in the presence of his brothers, he anointed David *as the one God had chosen.* (The text does not reveal the purpose of the anointing.)

Smoldering resentment at God's rejection of him as King was building up in Saul's heart and tormenting him. His attendants recommended that he find someone who could play the harp, so that when this tormenting spirit came upon him, the music would soothe him. One of Saul's servants had heard David, the son of Jesse, play the harp in Bethlehem and told King

Saul about it. Saul sent for David, and David's music pleased him very much (16:22). King Saul then asked Jesse, David's father, to let his son remain in the king's service. David traveled back and forth, tending his father's sheep at home, and serving King Saul at his bidding. The three oldest sons of Jesse were serving in Saul's army at that time.

One day Jesse sent David with food for his three brothers, and that is when David learned of the Philistine giant, Goliath. David's slaying of this giant elevated respect for him in the minds of his fellow soldiers; and women sang songs that praised David (17:1 – 58). But the words they used to praise David definitely demonstrated that King Saul was far behind the young soldier in popularity. This was the beginning of Saul's jealousy of David. Two evils were developing in Saul's heart, resentment for being rejected as king, and now, jealousy of David as a warrior. Saul nurtured these toxic feelings and they were poisoning his heart (18:6 – 9).

From that time forward, Saul became obsessed with jealousy and hatred. He began an unrelenting campaign to rid himself of this popular warrior. One day, while David was singing for Saul, the King threw a spear at him which lodged in the wall. David knew then that the King was planning to kill him. He fled from place to place to escape the King's wrath.

Saul, learning David was in the desert of En Gedi, took 3000 soldiers to search for him. Saul went into a cave to relieve himself, not knowing that David and his men were deep inside. When they learned that Saul was in the cave, David's soldiers rejoiced that God had delivered the enemy into David's hands. David then slipped up behind Saul and secretly cut off a corner of his robe. He had the opportunity to take the life of his king, but he did not – because *it was God who had chosen Saul to be king* (1 Samuel 24:1 – 4).

Remember, God gave the Israelites a king according to their own wishes. What the people wanted was very different from what they should have asked God to give them. In spite of this, *David still considered Saul to be the anointed king,* **chosen by God.** When Saul realized how David had spared his life, he wept, acknowledging that David had been merciful. He admitted that David would be king and begged him not to destroy his family or his family name (1 Samuel 24:19 – 21).

David would not harm the one God had chosen; neither did he take the life of any of Saul's sons. But in spite of Saul's conciliatory words to David from a distance away, Saul continued to hate David, pursuing him with his 3000 soldiers, trying again to kill him. Later, David had another opportunity to kill Saul.

One night, while Saul was camped with his soldiers, thinking that David was nowhere near, the king and all his men settled into sleep for the night. David, with his 600 men, had scouts to watch the movement of Saul's army and they reported to David. David asked for someone to go with him into Saul's camp and Abishai volunteered. (Enoch's Navy training tells him that Saul committed a huge military mistake by not having his camp guarded adequately all through the night.)

They entered Saul's camp undetected and found Saul and Abner sound asleep with many soldiers sleeping all around. Saul's spear was stuck in the ground near his head with his water jug nearby. Abishai offered to use the spear and *pin him to the ground with one thrust of the spear.* David restrained Abishai and told him that Saul was still the one God had chosen; no one could harm him without guilt. David took Saul's spear and water jug as they left the camp. The text states that God had put all the soldiers into a deep sleep. Read it all in 1 Samuel 26:2 – 12.

After David and Abishai had retreated some distance away, they roused the sleeping camp. Saul realized it was David, and that he had once again spared his life.

1 Samuel 26:21, 25

21 Then Saul said, "I have sinned.
Come back, David my son.
Because you considered my life precious today,
I will not try to harm you again. Surely I have
acted like a fool, and have erred greatly . . . ."

25 Then Saul said to David,
"May you be blessed, my son David;
you will do great things and surely triumph."
So David went on his way, and Saul returned home.

David's absolute respect for the choice God had made is shown, not only by his refusal to kill Saul, but also by his patience in waiting for **God to act in His way** to end the reign of King Saul. This is one of the many reasons the Hebrew writer included David among the *Great Cloud of Witnesses* in chapter 11. But there is much more to learn about David's trust in God, and his desire to honor Him.

THE SCENE CHANGES

Bailiff: *Please present*

David, the Second King of Israel

The name of David is found in the Old Covenant over 1000 times, and more than fifty times in the New. David called upon the Lord for strength and guidance many times, an example for all of us. Saul perished in a battle and his two healthy sons died in the same war. David became the King and his first task was to unite all the tribes that had descended from Jacob, then and now known as the Children of Israel.

From early childhood, we have heard the story of David and Goliath many times. It seems that the focus was always on the bravery of David. However, on reading the text again and again over the years, we have come to realize that David's great courage came from his trust in God. He strongly believed that there was no enemy, not even the giant, Goliath, who could prevail over God's people (1 Samuel 17). Saul was rejected as king because *he* did not listen carefully to all of God's words. On the other hand, David completely trusted everything God said – a huge difference between Saul and David.

God gave David rest after the many battles he had to fight for his position of strength as the king of all Israel. The task God had given David was to unify the descendants of Abraham through Jacob (Israel) into one nation, a people of God's own possession. After attaining this power, it was quite reasonable for David to build a king's palace; that was what kings did! However, David had other building ideas which we will learn about in Chapter Six.

The Psalms David composed also reveal the depth of his trust in God.

o o o o o

Bailiff: *Please present*

A Few of David's Psalms

In Psalm 3, David prays for God's protection, for himself and all of Israel.

Psalm 3:3, 4, 8

3 But you, Lord, are a shield around me,
my glory, the One who lifts my head high.

4 I call out to the Lord,
and he answers me from his holy mountain.

8 From the Lord comes deliverance.
May your blessing be on your people.

Psalm 8 not only tells us how much David truly believed in God, but it also echoes many of the things we have already discussed.

Psalm 8:1 – 9

1 LORD, our Lord,
how majestic is your name in all the earth!
You have set your glory
in the heavens.

2 Through the praise of children and infants
you have established a stronghold against your enemies,
to silence the foe and the avenger.

3 When I consider your heavens,
the work of your fingers,
the moon and the stars,
which you have set in place,

4 what is mankind that you are mindful of them,
human beings that you care for them?

5 You have made them a little lower than the angels
and crowned them with glory and honor.
6 You made them rulers over the works of your hands;
you put everything under their feet:

7 all flocks and herds,
and the animals of the wild,

8 the birds in the sky,
and the fish in the sea,
all that swim the paths of the seas.
9 LORD, our Lord,
how majestic is your name in all the earth!

David is amazed, *as we should be,* at the magnificence of the Created Universe, and he outlines the responsibilities all human beings have in relation to all other life forms. Let us all say to God, **how majestic is your name in all the earth!**

Psalm 15:1 – 5

1 LORD, who may dwell in your sacred tent?
Who may live on your holy mountain?

The answer to these two questions identifies the choices that all of us must make on a day by day basis. The struggle between good and evil, between right and wrong, and between obedience and disobedience, has been with us since Adam and Eve! In fact, the struggle between these opposing forces has been going on in all parts of the world for thousands of years. It is not something new for people on earth to have to deal with. The answer to those two questions describes the kind of person everyone would deeply appreciate having as a friend.

2 The one whose walk is blameless,
who does what is righteous,
who speaks the truth from their heart;

3 whose tongue utters no slander,
who does no wrong to a neighbor,
and casts no slur on others;

*4 who despises a vile person
but honors those who fear the LORD;
who keeps an oath even when it hurts,
and does not change their mind;*

*5 who lends money to the poor without interest;
who does not accept a bribe against the innocent.
Whoever does these things
will never be shaken.*

We know that we cannot be **fully blameless,** but that must be our goal. We know that we cannot always do **what is righteous,** but we must make the choice to try. David has identified the kinds of choices that we must make every day: always speaking the truth, despising and avoiding all kinds of evil, showing kindness toward all other people, honoring those **who fear the Lord,** and making every effort to please our Father in heaven. David's trust in God is clearly revealed when he confidently states, **Whoever does these things will never be shaken.**

Psalm 19:14

Faith in and devotion to God are intertwined. David expressed this beautifully in this verse which has been a prayer in faithful hearts for thousands of years.

*May these words of my mouth
and this meditation of my heart
be pleasing in your sight,
LORD, my Rock and my Redeemer.*

Psalm 25:4 – 5

This plea of David could not be made without complete trust in the answer that God would give him. He is asking for God to teach him His paths and for God to guide him in His truth, and he proclaims God as his Savior.

4 Show me your ways, LORD,
teach me your paths.

5 Guide me in your truth and teach me,
for you are God my Savior,
and my hope is in you all day long.

It is good to ask God in prayer to **show me His ways;** to **teach me His paths;** to **allow His truth to guide me;** to **recognize that God is my Savior;** to **keep my hope in God all day long.** This is a call to give ourselves completely into God's control.

Psalm 23:1 – 6

No one knows how old David was when he wrote this, but Psalm 23 is now known all over the world. Confidence in the truth of what is written is evident throughout the Psalm, and that confidence is based on the life experiences of David himself. It is our hope that these comments *will not detract* from this powerful message.

1 The LORD is my shepherd, I lack nothing.

David was a shepherd himself, the youngest of the eight sons of Jesse. He risked his own life to protect the sheep under his care. But in this Psalm he places himself as a sheep and the Lord God of Heaven as **The Shepherd.**

2 He makes me lie down in green pastures,
he leads me beside quiet waters,

3 he refreshes my soul.

Good pasture land and clear, clean water are essential for the health of the sheep. David had complete confidence that God provides all needed things. In the next verse, David expresses another quality of a good shepherd; he must take the sheep along paths that are not dangerous for any of them. He finds these safe paths because he wants to be known as a good shepherd. God is our Good Shepherd, and offers to be *that Good Shepherd for all who freely come to Him.*

He guides me along the right paths for his name's sake.

There have always been dark valleys, even valleys of death, in our world. David was confident that God would bring him safely through the darkest places. The shepherd's staff, with its rod (crook), served to guide and protect the sheep; David spoke his own language to describe how God's guidance and protection brought comfort to his heart.

**4 Even though I walk
through the darkest valley,
I will fear no evil,
for you are with me;
your rod and your staff,
they comfort me.**

Verse 5 shows how confident David was that God, the Great Shepherd, could prepare a meal for David in the very presence of enemies. To have such a faith as David's requires that we keep our eyes fixed on God, fixed on Jesus, the Good Shepherd of our souls.

**5 You prepare a table before me
in the presence of my enemies.
You anoint my head with oil;
my cup overflows.**

The conclusion of this great Psalm begins with the word *surely.* It then proclaims the very nature of God, *goodness and love.* David is confident God will be with him all the days of his life. And David is also convinced that he will dwell in the house of the Lord forever.

6 Surely your goodness and love will follow me
all the days of my life,
and I will dwell in the house of the LORD forever.

CHAPTER SIX

Evidence from the prophets Aaron, Moses, Deborah, Samuel, Nathan, Elijah, Elisha

Me: *Your honor, The Old Covenant*
tells of many prophets
and their prophecies. I would like to present details
for some of the more prominent ones,
but briefs for a few others.
It is the accuracy of their foretelling
that strengthens faith.
Judge: *Bailiff, please call the prophets.*

Bailiff: *The Prophet Aaron*

God called Moses to lead the children of Israel out of slavery in Egypt, but because Moses made excuses for not being an eloquent speaker, God appointed his brother, Aaron, to be his spokesperson and prophet (Exodus 7:1ff).

o o o o o

Bailiff: *The Prophet Moses*

We have already written about Moses as one of *That Great Cloud of Witnesses,* but Moses was charged by God to do many things. For example, he made a Messianic prophecy that one like himself would come. He clearly said that all must listen to that One, meaning the Messiah, Jesus (Deuteronomy 18:15). But Moses also prophesied many things about the children of Israel throughout their forty years of wandering in the wilderness. These examples of his faith in God can be found in Exodus, Leviticus, Numbers, and Deuteronomy. In our next chapter we will focus on an amazing prophecy recorded by Moses in Deuteronomy 28, where the history of the Jewish people is outlined for a period of about 1500 years, to the destruction of Jerusalem in A.D. 70.

o o o o o

Bailiff: *The Prophet Deborah*

Deborah was both a prophet and a judge in Israel (Judges 4:4ff). Her specific prophecy concerned Barak, of whom we have already written. Many of this great *Cloud of the Prophets of Israel* also made prophecies that were fulfilled in a short time. However, our goal is to realize that no prophecy could be accurate without God's revelation to the prophet. Our faith is strengthened as we see how each prophet spoke the truth, which could come only by the guidance of God.

o o o o o

Bailiff: *The Prophet Samuel*

We have already written about Samuel as one of the *Great Cloud of Witnesses* mentioned in Hebrews 11. For further study, read these two prophecies Samuel made concerning the children of Israel: I Sam 3:20, 21; and 9:17 – 20. Note: The term "seer" means a prophet. Gad was a "seer" for David, that is, one who received messages from God to give to David. Both terms are used in 2 Samuel 24:11. You will find many examples of Samuel as a prophet in 1 Samuel.

○ ○ ○ ○ ○

Bailiff: *The Prophet Nathan*

We have great respect for the courage of Nathan, the prophet, who not only prophesied about the events of Israel, but particularly prophesied events concerning that great king of Israel, David. Nathan told the truth in every circumstance, even to King David, who had the power to take his life. In 2 Samuel 7:1 – 17 we learn how God used both David and Nathan to do His will. We also learn how sincerely both David and Nathan trusted in the message from God.

David, in the custom of kings, built himself a palace of cedar, and then thought that he should also build a palace for God. He told the prophet Nathan what he had in mind, and Nathan told him to go ahead, *The LORD is with you* (v. 2). But that night, the Lord spoke to Nathan and gave him a message for David.

God reminded David that He had been traveling with the Israelites everywhere. God had never asked the leaders, whom He had appointed, the question, *"Why have you not built me a house of cedar?"* God reviewed David's history, how he, a shepherd of sheep, had been chosen to become the King of Israel. God reminded David that He had always been with him in every battle, and he promised that David's name would be as great as that of any king on earth. God also promised that David's own flesh and blood, not David, would build the house for God. Nathan reported to David *all the words of this entire revelation* (v. 17).

One part of this revelation to Nathan was a promise that scholars may consider as applying to the Messiah. God had said, *But my love will never be taken away from him, as I took it away from Saul* (v. 15). Whether it was referring especially to the continuing reign of the line of David, or was foretelling God's faithfulness to the Messiah, may not be clearly known. The concept surely applies to both.

Iit is commendable that David, after building a house of cedar for himself as king, wanted to build something for *God to live in.* But did David understand the nature of God so well that he could build a structure suitable for the Creator of the Universe? It is our judgment that David just felt good about his own palace and, in appreciation for all the blessings God had given him for so long, he wanted to do something "great" for God. What David believed about where God Himself lived is not known, but It is very obvious that David wanted to honor God. However, we do need to face the question, *Where does God live?*

Luke, Paul, and Peter tell us interesting things which will help us understand more about the nature of God. Luke tells us what Paul said to the Athenians, *God does not live in temples made by the hands of men* (Acts 17:24). On closer study, we know the Temple, built in Jerusalem, was to be a place where all Jewish believers could come to offer sacrifices to God, and celebrate other special events in Jewish history. There is no teaching that places God only in that temple and nowhere else. Paul also describes where God desires to live, and it is located all over the earth, wherever people seek God on His terms and come to Him in obedient faith. Paul, in Ephesians 2, said, in essence, that God wants to live in *willing human hearts – that is the temple God desires to live in!* The location is not in any physical building, but in the hearts of those people who come to God through Jesus.

Peter opens our eyes to another attribute of God, He is timeless. He said . . . *With the Lord a day is like a thousand years, and a thousand years are like a day* (2 Peter 3:8).

These passages help us know more of the eternal nature of God, but if God does not live in buildings made by the hands of men, why did God allow David's son Solomon to build a temple? Remember, this "building" began as a tent! This tent was the tabernacle in which God allowed His people to bring offerings to Him, and be instructed by the priests. *Meeting His people in the "tent of meeting" did not limit God in any way.* However, it did begin a pattern of community, of bringing people together for a common purpose – **to praise, honor, and worship God – together.**

The nature of God encompasses many things: His great power, *omnipotence;* His great knowledge, *omniscience;* His abiding presence, *omnipresence;* His love for all people, *God Himself is love;* His hatred of evil, yet *He desires to save all those lost in evil.* We can learn much about God's nature as we study, passage by passage, event by event, from God's word. However, we *must read and study with an open mind.*

From the very beginning, God has wanted those created in His image to know Him, to know His nature. He is the Creator who gives us life. He is the Creator of the universe. With the words of the prophets of Israel, God helps us understand who He is, and how He cares for all people. The more we realize His patience, and understand how He has always wanted to develop a relationship with His "creatures," the stronger our own faith becomes.

The background of the next prophecy of Nathan is found in 2 Samuel 11, where we read a tragic story of King David. One night, David got up from his bed and took a walk on his palace roof. He saw, perhaps unintentionally, a beautiful woman bathing. Human desire took over and David sent for the woman, took her to his bed, then sent her home. After a short while, Bathsheba let David know that she was pregnant. This created a problem for David, a big problem. The husband of Bathsheba was Uriah, the Hittite, a soldier in the service of King David!

Even King David, who trusted God with all his heart, fell prey to an all too common human weakness. Like most of us, he immediately tried to cover his wrong-doing. He sent for Uriah to come back home for a few days, obviously intending for Uriah to have relations with his wife. But the loyalty of Uriah for his commander, Joab, his fellow soldiers, **and for his king,** was very strong. He did not go to his own home but slept outside all night in the entrance to the palace with the servants of the king. Why did he not go to his home and see his wife? Loyalty is a very commendable character trait, but the loyalty of Uriah made David's plan to cover up his own sin very difficult. So David tried again.

Most of us have heard the expression, "one sin leads to another and then to another." To solve his worsening dilemma, David tried to get Uriah drunk so that he would go home and be with his wife, Bathsheba. *But he still would not go home.* In desperation, David sent Uriah back to the battlefront with instructions to the commander to put Uriah in the thick of battle and then withdraw. Uriah, the loyal servant of the King, was killed – because of the specific instructions of the King. David plunged from fulfilled lust, to attempted cover-up, to blatant deception, and finally, to cold-bloodied murder.

In the vile culture of today, all of us have much to learn from the consequences David had to face from his own sins. If King David, with all his great trust in God, can be conquered by a sinful desire, then who are we to ignore the ever-present danger of that temptation? *All ignored temptations are dangerous!* We must daily choose to do good, not evil; choose the right and never the wrong – *for as long as we live!*

Again, God uses Nathan the prophet to bring about a solution to this terrible situation. In this case, God gave Nathan a parable to tell David.

2 Samuel 12:1 – 4

1 The LORD sent Nathan to David.
When he came to him, he said,
"There were two men in a certain town,
one rich and the other poor.
2 The rich man had a very large
number of sheep and cattle,
3 but the poor man had nothing
except one little ewe lamb
he had bought. He raised it, and it grew
up with him and his children.
It shared his food, drank from his cup
and even slept in his arms.
It was like a daughter to him.
4 Now a traveler came to the rich man,
but the rich man refrained
from taking one of his own sheep or
cattle to prepare a meal for the
traveler who had come to him. Instead,
he took the ewe lamb that
belonged to the poor man and prepared it
for the one who had come to him."

When David heard of the cruelty and greed of the rich man, he **burned with anger,** and was prepared to punish him for this horrible injustice. Imagine his astonishment when Nathan said, *You are the man! This is what the Lord, the God of Israel, said . . . Why did you despise the word of the Lord by doing what is evil in his eyes? You struck down Uriah, the Hittite with the sword and took his wife to be your own. You killed him with the sword of the Ammonites* (2 Samuel 12:7, 9).

David was penitent and God forgave him, but there were shock-waves that followed David's moral earthquake. Nathan told the King that because of his sin, he had **made the enemies** *of the Lord show utter contempt* (v. 14). Before Nathan left David, he prophesied unhappy events that would come to David and his household; the death of Bathsheba's child was foretold. Among Nathan's parting words was this chilling prophecy.

2 Samuel 12:10

Now, therefore, the sword will never
depart from your house,
because you despised me
and took the wife of Uriah the Hittite to be your own.

This prophecy, *the sword will never depart from your house,* reveals that God knew what David had done; there is no escape from the consequences of any sin. It also shows that God knows the desires of our bodies and He wants us to **control those desires** *all the time!* We do not know how long it was after this tragedy when David wrote Psalm 51, but reading his words and hearing his pain, we can know how to be humbly penitent for our sins. David did not try to hide his sins from the face of God. How do we stand before God when we know we have sinned? Do we have the courage to confess that sin specifically to God?

As the two of us get older, the more we realize just how much forgiveness God grants to us, and how much He loves us in spite of our sins. That is the very nature of God – *His love, His mercy, His forgiveness,* for which *Jesus paid the price –* **He forgives us!** No wonder our gratitude for His forgiveness increases day by day!

o o o o o

Bailiff: *The Prophet Elijah*

Many prophets and leaders served God faithfully in Old Testament times. How could we know who is most important in God's eyes? Perhaps what Jesus did with Peter, James, and John will give us some understanding. Jesus took them up on a mountain where, before their very eyes, He was transformed into a vision of bright light, and Moses and Elijah were present talking with Jesus. Perhaps this will help us know the importance of Elijah in God's scheme of things. Our observation is not to take away from Isaiah, Jeremiah, or any of the other great prophets of God, but we need to know the importance of Elijah in Jewish thinking (Matthew 17:1 – 3).

It is significant that from all the Old Covenant leaders, prophets, and priests, only Elijah and Moses appeared with Jesus on that mountain. In the minds of the Jewish people, Elijah truly held a very important place as a prophet of Israel. When we look at a few of his experiences, we will see a prophet of strong faith and trust in God.

Elijah did not prophesy good news to King Ahab, but warned him there would be no rain for the next few years, *unless the prophet called for it* (1 Kings 17:1). Ahab did not want to hear such words, and probably became very angry. Elijah thought his life was in danger and ran away. God told him how to escape the wrath of Ahab, telling him to hide east of the Jordan in a ravine. That seems strange – what about food? There he had a brook for water and God ordered the ravens to feed him there (1 Kings 17:4).

We do not know how the ravens brought the food to Elijah for weeks or even months of time! But they did, and Elijah survived in that ravine. When the brook dried up, God told Elijah to go to the home of a poor widow. He had already commanded the widow to give food to Elijah, but she had only enough for herself and her son. Elijah told her to prepare some bread first for him and then make a meal for herself and her son.

How deep and complete was the faith of Elijah! He had confronted Ahab with an unwelcome truth. He had fled from the wrath of Ahab, trusting God for protection and guidance. When the brook dried up, he immediately obeyed God and went to the widow's home.

How deep and complete was the faith of the widow! She knew that God had commanded her to feed the prophet, but God made no promise to her. When Elijah told her to prepare food first for him, and then for herself and her son, she did not hesitate. She did what God had commanded. She trusted God even though she knew she and her family were facing starvation.

Then God did another amazing thing: He did not allow either the flour or the cooking oil to diminish for the remaining time of the drought. God saw to the safety of His prophet and had compassion for this poor widow and her son (1 Kings 17).

God then sent Elijah to appear before Ahab and challenge the power of the idols and their prophets. The amazing faith of Elijah is evident as he confronted Ahab and the many prophets of Baal. Elijah had complete trust in everything that God revealed to him, and he carried out each command enthusiastically. The best illustration of this kind of faith is a very unusual contest on Mount Carmel.

King Ahab wanted to kill Elijah because every prophecy he gave to the King was not what he wanted to hear. But God intended for Elijah to face Ahab and all his prophets in a most unusual contest. Obadiah was an official in charge of King Ahab's palace, but was very loyal to God. He had hidden one hundred prophets of God in two caves, feeding them and keeping them safe from Ahab and his Queen (1 Kings 18:4). Elijah happened to meet up with Obadiah and asked him to go to Ahab and say, **Elijah is coming to see you**. Obadiah was stunned by Elijah's request; he was afraid that Ahab would kill him. But his faith was strong enough; he did go to King Ahab and deliver Elijah's message.

The confrontation took place in Ahab's court. Ahab wanted to get rid of Elijah, as did Jezebel, his wife. She also hated Elijah and had killed many of the Lord's prophets. Ahab met with Elijah and called him a trouble-maker, but Elijah replied that the trouble for Israel was coming from Ahab's family, accusing him of bowing down to idols. Elijah immediately called for Ahab to bring together the 450 prophets of Baal and the 400 prophets of Asherah who were fed at the table of Jezebel. In addition, Elijah called for all the people and all the prophets to meet on Mt. Carmel (full text 1 Kings 18).

Elijah told the people that they could no longer continue trying to live with two different choices; they had to decide whether the Lord is God, or Baal is God. The people did not answer. The prophet of the Lord and the prophets of Baal began to make complex preparations for a spectacular contest. Two sacrificial bulls were chosen. The prophets of Baal cut up their bull and placed it on the wood of their altar. Neither Elijah nor Baal's prophets were to set fire to the wood.

The real contest began as Elijah told the prophets of Baal to call for their god to send fire down and consume their offering. They began with shouts and dancing until noon with no response. Elijah began to taunt them because there was no answer from Baal, so they shouted louder and began to cut themselves in their frenzy of appeals – still no response from their god. Time for the evening sacrifice had come.

Elijah then repaired the neglected altar of the Lord, cut up the other bull, placed it on the wood, then dug a trench around the altar. Next came a most unusual thing – Elijah called *for much water* to be poured on the bull, the wood, and all the altar, filling the trench. Then Elijah began his supplication to God.

1 Kings 18:36 – 39

36 At the time of sacrifice, the prophet Elijah stepped forward and prayed: "LORD, the God of Abraham, Isaac and Israel,

let it be known today that you are God
in Israel and that I am your
servant and have done all these things at your command.

37 Answer me, LORD, answer me, so
these people will know that you,
LORD, are God, and that you are turning
their hearts back again."

38 Then the fire of the LORD fell and
burned up the sacrifice, the wood,
the stones and the soil, and also licked
up the water in the trench.

39 When all the people saw this,
they fell prostrate and cried,
"The LORD—he is God! The LORD—he is God!"

God then had Elijah to put to death all these false prophets, of both Baal and the Asherah poles. This was reported by Ahab to Jezebel, who vowed to kill *that troubler of Israel.* However, as they left Mount Carmel, Elijah told Ahab to get in his chariot because a great rain was coming (ending a drought of three and a half years). At the word of Elijah, the rains did come, but he was still afraid of Ahab.

Our purpose is not to tell the full story of these prophets of Israel, but to focus on their amazing faith in God. Much more could be told about Elijah, his prophecies and his faith, but there is no question about his full trust in what God told him to do. He is a great example for us to follow. There is a little more to tell about Elijah, but first, let us read an interesting article about prophets.

Throughout the writings of the Kings and Chronicles, there are many other prophets mentioned, often without giving their names, just **a man of God spoke.** What is the nature of all these prophecies? Dr. Don Kinder, in his introduction to our Bible class on Isaiah, listed seven things these various prophets did. His list is printed here with his kind permission. The comments to follow will have a reference number (from these 7) for the reader's convenience.

Remind me – What is a PROPHET?

1. Someone who prophesies.
2. They "forth-tell" more than they "fore-tell."
3. Their messages are tough.
4. They received the Lord's messages in various ways.
5. Many messages were Warnings (as from "watchmen").
6. They also preached Hope oracles.
7. Their messages were relevant to that time period.

(The above is from class notes from Dr. Don Kinder, June 23, 2019. Dr. Kinder credits his own notes from a class taught by Dr. John T. Willis. Dr. Willis used his own text, *My Servants, the Prophets,* Volume One, pages 5 – 6, Abilene, Texas: Biblical Research Press, 1971.)

A prophet does much more than predict the future (1). He may also give a warning (5), or give hope (6), or simply proclaim a message (7). He also may describe something that the Messiah will do when He comes (and Jesus fulfilled every prophecy made by all the prophets in both Covenants). Both Elijah and Elisha predicted things that would happen in the immediate future (2), not just something that would happen many centuries later, as many of the Old Covenant prophets did. How tough (3) were some of these prophecies? Here are two examples: Saul would lose the kingship by death; Ahab's whole family would die and no future king would come through his bloodline. The suffering of the Messiah, as so accurately described in Isaiah 53, is surely a "tough" prophecy, not only for the Messiah, of course, but also for the Jewish people.

Many could not accept the idea of a Messiah coming from the "common" people, and certainly a crucified Messiah was not to be considered.

God used various ways to communicate (4) to His prophets: dreams, visions, angels as messengers, a burning bush, handwriting on a wall, to list a few. His Word, understood in its context, communicates to us today, if we will listen to it and absorb His message. But in almost every instance, those who heard the prophet speak knew how it applied to them (7), even if it meant something to come to pass later and not immediately.

Thank you, Dr. Kinder for your input. It will help all of us as readers of God's word to grasp a fuller meaning of the words, faith, and actions of these prophets.

All of the prophets had great trust in what God revealed to them, most all of whom had prophesied about something to do with the people of Israel. However, we will tell of another **Great Cloud** when we write of the prophets of the Messiah.

Me: *Your Honor, there is some*
overlapping in the lives of the
two prophets, Elijah and Elisha. May
I deal with this as a transition
period and then present Elisha as the next prophet?
Judge: *That is a reasonable request.*
You may proceed. Let the
Bailiff call Elisha at the proper time.
Me: *Thank you, your Honor.*

The Transition from Elijah to Elisha

Elijah believed he was the only prophet left in Israel and asked God to take his life (1 Kings 19:4). In reply, God showed him there were 7000 in Israel who had not bowed down to Baal, nor kissed his image (19:18). God had told Elijah to find Elisha and appoint him to be his successor as prophet (19:16). This he did and Elisha, who had been plowing with a team of oxen, said goodbye to his parents, sacrificed his oxen, and became the attendant to Elijah (19:19 – 21). (Today, we would say Elisha was serving as an apprentice to Elijah.)

Both Elijah and Macaiah, another prophet of God, spoke words to Ahab which he did not want to hear: telling him how he and his wife, Jezebel, would die (1 Kings 22). The pronouncement against Ahab and his descendants was clear. After Ahab died, Ahaziah, his son, became King of Israel. But after two years he died, leaving no son to ascend the throne. The prophetic words of Elijah were fulfilled to the letter.

It seems strange that Ahab and all the others who rejected the God who had led them out of slavery, and had taken care of them for hundreds of years, *could not see* – those reliable words could come only from the prophets who were instructed by the God of Heaven and earth.

How often do we today suffer the consequences of our evil choices and do not even consider looking for something better? Can we criticize the people of that time when we have the same problem in our own culture? We are personally acquainted with a person who has made wrong choices for dozens of years. That person seems unable to recognize that the suffering came from the consequences of those wrong choices. Blaming someone else for one's wrong choices is denying reality.

Ahaziah followed in his father's ways, and when he was injured from a fall, he sent for the prophets of Baal to ask if he would survive his injuries. It was Elijah who came on the scene to tell him that he would not leave his bed alive, *and he did not, just as Elijah had spoken* (2 Kings 1).

As preparations were made for God to take Elijah, several interesting things occurred. When Elijah and Elisha were together in Gilgal, the old prophet said, **Stay here; the Lord has sent me to Bethel.** Elisha said he would go with him. In Bethel, the company of prophets met Elisha and said to him, **Do you know that the Lord is going to take your master** *from you today?* Elisha said he did, but he did *not want to talk about it.* Then the two men went to Jericho and on to the Jordan river; Elisha would not leave Elijah (2 Kings 2).

Just before God took Elijah to be with Him, Elijah asked Elisha, *Tell me, what can I do for you before I am taken from you?* Elisha replied, *Let me inherit a double portion of your spirit* (2 Kings 2:9). Elijah told him that if he saw him as he was taken up, then his request would be granted. Elisha did see Elijah as God took him up – *in a chariot of fire with fiery horses in a whirlwind* (2:11). The things Elisha did after Elijah left are clear evidence that Elisha had God's Spirit in him as a prophet of God.

How great was the trust of both men in what God did! The prophets they met in Bethel and Jericho knew that God was going to take Elijah (2 Kings 2). How did all these people know this? God must have revealed to them that this most unusual, never-before-seen event was about to happen.

Elisha knew where God was taking Elijah, but the company of prophets at Jericho did not. Even after witnessing this amazing spectacle, *a horse-drawn chariot of fire, taking Elijah up into the sky*, the prophets in Jericho still begged Elisha to let them send fifty able men to search the mountains and valleys for Elijah. At first Elisha refused their request, but finally relented and told them to send their men. For three days they looked everywhere, but could not find Elijah. Elisha simply said, " . . . *Didn't I tell you not to go?"* (2 Kings 2:18).

Is there a line drawn between faith in what God says He will do, and actual knowledge of what God planned to do? No one can come to "know God" fully – that is beyond human ability – but with so much evidence, confidence grows and becomes a definite feeling of *Yes, God is real! I know without doubt.* May the study of these witnesses increase the faith of each one of us who reads and thinks deeply about these texts. How beautiful to see so many people responding in trust to God's word!

○ ○ ○ ○ ○

Bailiff: *The Prophet Elisha*

Elisha followed in the footsteps of Elijah in many ways. The interesting thing is that many of the acts of these two prophets were very similar to what Jesus did. Warnings to the leadership, compassionate care for the sick, and even raising the dead were events in the lives of these two prophets – even more so in the life of Jesus.

Turning our focus now to Elisha, we see that his attitude toward the poor and needy shows just how much the spirit of Jesus was in his heart. Our study of a few of these events will come from the Book of 2 Kings.

When the people became sick from drinking water from the springs that served the community, God helped Elisha purify the water, and it stayed clean (2:19 – 22). When forty-two youth made fun of the bald-headed Elisha, God protected him by sending a bear to maul these unruly young people (2:23 – 25).

The king of Moab rebelled against the kings of Judah, Israel, and Edom. Because Jehoshaphat wanted to seek the guidance of the Lord before going to war, Elisha **did seek** the counsel of God on their behalf (3:1 – 27).

God gave Elisha many ways to solve the problems of people. The scriptures, in 2 Kings 4:1 – 7, reveal an unusual way to solve a widow's problem. The wife of a deceased prophet came to Elisha crying for help. Her husband had a creditor demanding payment or else he would come and take her two sons to settle the debt, intending to make slaves of them. Elisha offered to help, then asked what she had in her house. She replied that she had only a small jar of olive oil. Then Elisha gave this widow some strange instructions: go to her neighbors and gather as many *empty jars* as she could find. Elisha also told her to close the door to her house *and pour oil into the empty jars!*

The widow did what Elisha told her to do, and many empty jars were brought to her home. She did this because she trusted the word of Elisha. More than that, she took her small jar of olive oil and began pouring oil into the other jars, another act of faith. After the jars were filled, she asked one of her two sons for more empty jars, but he said, "*there is not a jar left*." At that point, the oil from her small jar stopped flowing.

She went back and reported to Elisha, who told her the next thing to do, *"Go, sell the oil and pay your debts. You and your sons can live on what is left."* (4:7).

It was Elisha who told this widow what to do; it was God who caused the oil to continue to flow. We do not know what this woman thought about Elisha's instructions. We know she trusted Elisha's words because she sent her sons out to gather empty jars. They put them in her room and she closed the door. We do not know how she felt as she began to pour from her one small jar into the many – *but there was no hesitation in obeying the words of Elisha, God's prophet!*

Was she amazed that her jar could fill another, then another, until all of the many jars were full? God communicated to Elisha what to tell the widow to do, and Elisha did not question such a command. The complete trust in God by both Elisha and the widow *is clearly demonstrated by what they did.* The compassion of God for this widow, whose deceased husband had been a member of that company of prophets of God (4:1), is also demonstrated by what took place.

There was a wealthy Shunammite woman who showed kindness to Elisha and provided a comfortable place for him to stay whenever he came to her town (4:8 - 37). She had no son and her husband was old. Elisha prophesied that she and her husband would have a son, but she found it difficult to believe. However, the prophet spoke the truth and she did have a son. Several years later the child became sick and died. His mother laid his body in the bed they had prepared for Elisha. By God's help, Elisha brought the young boy back to life. This is another example of the compassion of God for people, and He used His prophet, Elisha, to show His care for the child.

Not only did this woman truly believe that Elisha was a prophet of God, she also believed that Elisha could do something for her dead son. Why? Was it because it was Elisha who had prophesied that she, a barren woman, would bear a son? She spoke confidently, revealing that she believed Elisha could call for God to restore her son to life. Elisha went, prayed to the Lord, and the child's life was restored. By her actions, we know she had a strong faith, one that challenges us to trust God when in difficult times (2 Kings 4:8 – 37).

Naaman, the commander of the army of the King of Aram, had leprosy (2 Kings 5:1 – 19a). At that time leprosy was a very serious illness and no one knew how to heal a leper. However, in Naaman's house there was a slave girl who had been captured from among the Hebrew people. She told Naaman's wife, her mistress, that if he would go see the prophet in Samaria, he would be healed. That prophet was Elisha.

Naaman reported this to his master, the King of Aram, who told him to go; the King then prepared a letter for the King of Israel. Israel's King was shocked because he knew he had no power to cure leprosy. He tore his clothes, thinking the King of Aram was picking a quarrel with him. When Elisha heard of the king's actions, he told the king to send the man to him. Naaman went to see Elisha at his home, and called for him to come out to meet him, but Elisha simply sent his messenger out to tell him what to do.

2 Kings 5:10b

. . . "Go, wash yourself 7 times in
the Jordan, and your flesh
will be restored and you will be cleansed."

But Naaman went away angry, crying out that the rivers of Damascus were cleaner than anything in Israel. He left in a rage, but his servants approached him and asked, *If you had been told to do something great, would you have obeyed?* Naaman listened to the words of his servants, went to the Jordan River and dipped himself seven times. His leprosy was cured and his flesh became like that of a young boy. Because of this experience, Naaman realized that the God of Israel is the only true God. He wanted to offer gifts, but Elisha would accept nothing from Naaman.

Naaman's offer of a gift brings up very important concepts all of us need to think about. *What kind of gift can we mortals give to God to pay – value for value – for any blessing we might receive from God?* Truly, we are not able to pay, value for value, for any blessing from God.

We cannot pay the price for even one sin of the many we have committed! People sell their souls to Satan so cheap, often for temporary pleasure with never a thought for the consequences. When Satan owns us, bought at the cheapest price, how can we buy our souls back? Jesus asked the same question: **What can a man give in exchange for his soul?** Jesus implied that even if we owned the whole world, it would not be enough to "buy back" our souls (Mark 8:34 – 37). Only Jesus is able to redeem our souls from the grip of Satan – **and He did – with His own blood!**

It is only by the love, grace, and mercy of a Loving Creator that He offers us the forgiveness of our sins. God does not ask for anything, neither silver or gold, or lands, or livestock, or any other material thing to pay for our sins. **He has accepted the blood of Jesus in full payment.**

Are we aware of how precious it is for God to forgive our sins? What then does God expect of those who come penitently to Him? He asks us to be *living sacrifices;* to be children in His family, not slaves; and to be **children of light** to all the people around us. God asks that we obediently trust

Him, and do the good works He wants us to do day-by-day. *It is difficult for Satan to tempt a person who is busy doing good things for others.*

We are not told about the life of Naaman after he was healed of his leprosy. We do know this: God expects us to continue to be faithful to Him, to Jesus, and listen to all of His words of truth, for *they are our guide in all we do.*

Sometimes faith comes to people in spite of their desire not to do what the Lord's prophet told them to do. It is good that Naaman returned to the Jordan and dipped himself seven times in obedience to Elisha's instructions (2 Kings 5:13 – 19). Naaman vowed that he would never worship any other god but Israel's God. He immediately asked for permission, when accompanying the king of Aram to worship his idol, to bow down with his king. He asked to be forgiven for this, recognizing that he would have problems being faithful to God while in service to his king. Elisha's response to his request for forgiveness did not address his problem. When he said, **Go in peace,** he expressed sympathy for Naaman's dilemma, and could have meant that God would help him through such situations. **Go in peace** does not open the door for doing anything one might want to do without God's guidance.

Because God was with him and gave him guidance, Elisha was able to appoint kings, tell a king his kingship would end, and perform miracles for someone in need. His prophecies concerned the kingdom of Judah and Jerusalem, the kingdom of Israel, and the kings of Aram, and were fulfilled soon after he spoke them.

The faith of all God's prophets, and of those who trusted the words of these prophets, is of a quality that any believer can follow with confidence.

The Old Covenant has seventeen books of prophecy beginning with Isaiah and ending with Malachi. Very much could be written about each of these prophets. However, as in the situations of Elijah and Elisha, most of the words of these

Old Testament prophets dealt with the people around them. Some also prophesied about the kingdom united by David and the divided kingdoms of Judah and Israel. When you read about these other prophets, you will also see great faith to emulate.

The book of Psalms contains a number of passages that are, in effect, prophecies: some about the children of Israel, and some about the coming Messiah. We pray that all of us, **make the time** to explore more of these Old Covenant texts. Such reading and study will continue to develop a deeper faith.

The next chapter is a study of an amazing prophecy that Moses wrote in detail about Israel. It is in two parts. The first tells how blessed all Israel will be if they trust and obey the words and guidance of God. The second part describes the terrible consequences for Israel if they *do not listen and obey*. This whole prophecy provides a serious challenge for us to both hear and obey as *God's children of light.* That is what God expects all of us to do today . . . no, not just today, *but every day!*

CHAPTER SEVEN

Deuteronomy 28 – A Prophecy of Moses

Bailiff: *Present your introduction to this chapter.*

Deuteronomy 28 reveals the blessings for obedience and the terrible consequences for disobedience. Consistent obedience to God was a serious problem for the Israelites. This chapter tells of events that happened between three hundred and fourteen hundred years after Moses died. The horrendous destruction of Jerusalem in A.D. 70, which Moses predicted in such gruesome detail, is extremely frightening but it reveals the truth – *Only God could be so accurate over a period of that many years!*

The first fourteen verses of this awesome chapter tell how those who truly trust in the Lord for all of their lives will be blessed. In verses 36 and 37, Moses predicts that Israel would have a king, but that there would be trouble. And, in verses 49 – 57, Moses tells of the horrible suffering that came about before and during the destruction of Jerusalem in A.D. 70.

Bailiff: *Present your findings for*

Selections from Deuteronomy 28:1 – 14

Moses begins with these words, *If you fully obey the* *LORD your God and carefully follow all his commands.* This chapter begins with the conditional word, *if.* It is repeated several times in these fourteen verses. Notice these conditions: *If you fully obey the LORD your God,* and *carefully follow all his commands* (v. 1); *if you obey the LORD your God* (v. 2); *if you keep the commands of the LORD your God and walk in obedience to him* (v. 9); and, *If you pay attention to the commands of the LORD your God that I give you this day and carefully follow them* (v. 13). There is no way mankind can be acceptable to God without following His Truth, His teachings, and His commands. Moses summarizes how God feels about our relationship to God's words with verse 14, *Do not turn aside from any of the commands I give you today, to the right or to the left, following other gods and serving them.* Let us be sure to note that these conditions were not just for the Hebrews, but that these are eternal principles of God's heart, of God's expectations for mankind. What about the blessings, you ask?

Many more words were used to describe the blessings but they cover all aspects of human life. God promises that they will be blessed: whether they live in a city or out (v. 3); they will be blessed with children, abundant crops from the soil, and the produce of their livestock (v. 4); their food supply will be plentiful (v. 5); they will be blessed wherever they go (v. 6); and their enemies will not prevail over them (v. 7). Moses wrote more of the details of God's promise to those who *carefully follow all his commands* (v. 8 – 13).

God loves all people, Jew and Gentile, rich and poor, saints and sinners, and that is a powerful truth. But to ignore the conditions God set for the Israelites by this prophecy of Moses, *or those set by the Lord Jesus,* is very unwise – it negates the promises and blessings firmly connected to these conditions.

Remember what God, at the very beginning, said to the children of Israel through Moses: *If you fully obey the LORD your God and carefully follow all his commands I give you today* . . . . Is this something that God gave to the Children of Israel alone? Or, *is this one of God's eternal truths* that applies to anyone, anywhere, at any time? May we "pick and choose" which truths of God we want to live by? May we choose to ignore or rationalize some "inconvenient" truths? Do we still want to do certain things "our own way"? Is this the only time God mentioned this need to follow all of His commands?

What is God telling us here? Is it not something like this? *I will bless this way and that way, here and there, up and down, IF* . . . . God had promised great blessings to the Children of Israel, *but the promise was conditioned upon their faithful obedience.* During the time of the judges, the people's pattern of life was something like this: they worshiped and obeyed God and were blessed; they rejected God, worshiped idols, did evil, and suffered; cried to God for mercy, and were forgiven. Soon afterwards, they repeated the same cycle – over and over, again and again!

The God of creation, who made us in His own image, is a caring, loving, and merciful God. But all of us human beings must listen to God's wisdom and guidance. He urges us to trust Him, to trust His truth, to do His will, and become His children of light. Has God changed His "rules" for our generation? Does God look only to see how we come together to worship Him on Sunday? Does He care nothing about what we do or think all the rest of the time? We have positive things to learn from these fourteen verses; God has conditions for His blessings. Are we listening?

What if they did not listen and obey? What would happen? The consequences of disobedience described in Moses' words are heart-rending, and should cause all of us to face these warnings honestly. In every passage concerning destruction, the condemnation is to the ones who chose not to listen to God, not to obey. But when people choose to do evil, their families also suffer, as well as their neighbors and their friends. Evil is an insidious cancer that eats away at the heart. Is it contagious? Can peer pressure be so powerful that it cannot be resisted? What we can learn from this sobering chapter has very strong implications for our present generation.

○ ○ ○ ○ ○

Bailiff: *Presenting*

Deuteronomy 28:36 – 37

About 300 years before it happened, Moses prophesied that the people would demand a king.

> *36 The LORD will drive you and the*
> *king you set over you to a*
> *nation unknown to you or your*
> *ancestors. There you will worship*
> *other gods, gods of wood and stone.*
>
> *37 You will become a thing of horror,*
> *a byword and an object of ridicule among*
> *all the peoples where the LORD will drive you.*

Even before they had judges, Moses prophesied they would set a king over themselves. The **nation unknown to you** was Assyria (v. 36). Actually, the Israelites were carried off into slavery two times; the first occurred in the eighth century B.C. when the Northern Kingdom of Israel was taken into Assyrian captivity. The second was in the sixth century B.C. when Jerusalem and Judea were overrun and the temple was destroyed. Both situations were the result of sin and rebellion against God. Hoshea, the last King of Israel, ruled in Samaria. When Shalmanezer, King of Assyria, invaded Samaria, he put Hoshea in prison. Then he set a siege over Samaria for three years, capturing most of the able-bodied people to be made slaves in Assyria. (Read more details of this in 2 Kings 17.)

Shalmanezer also brought many of his own people to Samaria to govern the weaker Jewish people who had been left there. This led to intermarriage, creating enmity between the Jewish people in Jerusalem and the half-Jewish descendants in Samaria. That enmity continued and increased in bitterness even to the days of Jesus.

The capture of the people of Judah and Jerusalem is recorded in 2 Kings 25. The desecration of the temple treasures and worship instruments, the burning of the temple, important buildings and houses, and the destruction of the city walls are also recorded.

In verse 37 above, there is a concept that may apply not only to the Jewish people who were driven into captivity, but it may also apply to many generations of Jewish people since that time. Disobeying God has long-range consequences for whoever chooses that wrong path.

The City of Jerusalem and its Temple are destroyed a Second Time

After seventy years of captivity in Babylon, the Jews were allowed to return to Jerusalem and take the temple treasures with them. They rebuilt the walls and took forty-six years to rebuild the temple. The Babylonian Empire fell to the Persians, and they, in turn, were conquered by the Greeks under Alexander, the Great. After Alexander's death, the Romans rose to power. Herod had control of Jerusalem by 37 B.C. while Caesar Augustus was the Emperor. All the governors of Israel's provinces were appointed by Rome. By A.D. 70, the Romans had controlled Israel for 107 years.

Perhaps because the expectation the Jews had for the Messiah to drive the Romans back to Rome was so strong, they rejected Jesus and continued rebelling against Rome. This culminated in the terror revealed by Moses in his descriptive prophecy.

These words of Moses are very detailed and fully substantiated by the records of secular history. The prophecy describes great suffering when the people shifted their trust in God to trust in the protective walls around Jerusalem. Hunger is an extremely strong desire in each one of us, but few have ever been "tested" by it as the Jewish people were in A.D. 70.

Jews from many parts of the world had come to Jerusalem. They also took refuge behind those high and very strong walls that surrounded the city. Historians report over two million men, women, and children were inside those trusted walls. Verses 49 – 57 depict a horrifying scene.

> **49 The LORD will bring a nation**
> **against you from far away,**
> **from the ends of the earth, like an eagle swooping down,**
> **a nation whose language you will not understand,**
>
> **50 a fierce-looking nation without respect for**
> **the old or pity for the young.**
>
> **51 They will devour the young of your livestock and**
> **the crops of your land until you are destroyed.**
> **They will leave you no grain, new wine**
> **or olive oil, nor any calves**
> **of your herds or lambs of your**
> **flocks until you are ruined.**
>
> **52 They will lay siege to all the**
> **cities throughout your land**
> **until the high fortified walls in which you trust fall down.**
> **They will besiege all the cities throughout**
> **the land the LORD your God is giving you.**

*53 Because of the suffering your
enemy will inflict on you
during the siege, you will eat the fruit of the womb,
the flesh of the sons and daughters the
LORD your God has given you.*

*54 Even the most gentle and sensitive man among you
will have no compassion on his own brother or the wife
he loves or his surviving children,*

*55 and he will not give to one of them
any of the flesh of his children that he is eating.
It will be all he has left because of
the suffering your enemy
will inflict on you during the siege of all your cities.*

*56 The most gentle and sensitive woman among you—so
sensitive and gentle that she would not venture to touch
the ground with the sole of her foot—
will begrudge the husband
she loves and her own son or daughter*

*57 the afterbirth from her womb
and the children she bears.
For in her dire need she intends to eat them secretly
because of the suffering your enemy will inflict on you
during the siege of your cities.*

The Latin language of the Roman soldiers is not a Semitic language as are Hebrew and Aramaic, which Jesus and the common people spoke. Because of the conquests of Alexander the Great a few centuries before, Greek was the "language of the world." The barbaric actions of the Romans are described in verses 49 to 52. The writings of an eye-witness reveal many details that support the accuracy of Moses' prophecy.

Flavius Josephus, Historian, Eyewitness

You are probably familiar with the historian, Josephus. However, we need to know more about this man if we are going to understand the significance of him as an eyewitness of the destruction of Jerusalem, A.D. 70. He was named Joseph ben Matthias at birth. His father was a Levite, and thus Josephus served as a priest. (It is reported that his mother was a descendant of a Jewish priest who had also served as a Jewish king.)

Josephus had been a military general and was captured by the Romans in war. Evidently he was carried to Rome. He became an author, and is considered to have been writing to honor his own people and defend Judaism. He later became a Roman citizen, taking the name, Flavius Josephus. Later, he was commissioned to write a history of the Jewish people.

Even though the Jewish people did not trust Josephus, and many considered him a renegade, his writings reveal the deep respect he had for his own people and the Jewish faith. The war against Israel began under Vespasian with the conquering of towns and cities from the Mediterranean Sea to Tiberius in Galilee. When he was called to Rome to be Emperor, his son Titus became the commanding General of the Roman army in the war against Israel.

Josephus, knowing the power of the Roman forces and the impossibility of a Jewish victory in this conflict, tried to bring peace on at least two occasions. However, his efforts were fruitless. General Titus had offered to overlook all the troubles of the past – even the sedition the Jewish people had inflicted on the Romans – in order to end the terrible famine and senseless killing and bring peace, but the Jewish leaders rejected his offer. Soon after, General Titus received a horrifying report, which Josephus recorded.

An Israelite woman had killed her own infant son, cooked the flesh, ate half of it and offered the other half to the Roman soldiers who had been harassing her. They were unable to deal with such horror and reported to General Titus what had happened.

Appalled by what he heard, Titus denied any responsibility for what she had done. However, this seems to have been a turning point in his attitude toward the Jews; it caused him to say that such a nation should not be seen by the sun. He then ordered the total destruction of Israel.

It is heart-breaking to read about the terrible suffering of the people. They had put their trust in the physical walls of their city – and it failed miserably. Hundreds of thousands of men, women, and children died of starvation and disease. True, some died from the swords of the soldiers, and some died because of the atrocities of the local trouble-makers who pilfered and harassed their own people.

Moses predicted that the Children of Israel would have a king; three hundred years later they did. Moses predicted two captivities and they happened. Moses predicted the tragedy which occurred in A.D. 70. The accuracy of his words compels us to admit that only God could be so exact in foretelling these events. Our hearts are filled with awesome wonder!

Oh Heavenly Father, please forgive our sins of disobedience. We seek guidance from Your holy truth and pray that every choice we make, day by day, will be in full trust of Your word. We honor Jesus for the love He has for all people, and we pray that we will always choose to honor and do Your will in all things. In the name of Jesus.

CHAPTER EIGHT

The Birth, Early Childhood, Lineage of Jesus

Bailiff: *Please present your* Introduction to Cloud Three

A word of caution may be in order. If we look at only one or even two of these Messianic prophecies, we may not be able to overcome the critics who suggest other possibilities, or who may even claim that the passage is not a prophecy at all. Scholars tell us there are several hundred prophecies of the Messiah, and we are examining only a few. Remember, Jesus fulfilled *each and every one of **all** the prophecies.* Critics have tried, unsuccessfully, to find one prophecy which Jesus did **not** fulfill. Many people have experienced some of the suffering the Messiah had to face, for example, but no one else comes close to fulfilling every prophecy. Our task is to *let the texts do their own revealing of what the prophecy means and who fulfilled it accurately.*

Basically, other than Jesus, no person can fit the description of the conditions made plain in these prophetic words. True, Jesus suffered; other people suffer. Jesus was betrayed by a friend; other people have been betrayed by a friend. But – when you consider only a few of the other related prophecies, the number of qualifying "fulfillers" diminishes rapidly. Long before all the Messianic prophecies are examined, no one is left for consideration. The evidence that Jesus fulfilled all of these prophecies is powerfully persuasive, leaving no room for doubt. Examining the evidence for ourselves will strengthen our confident faith that *Jesus is the Christ, the Son of God!*

We are grateful for the list of thirty-eight prophecies in *The Thompson Chain Reference Bible,* found on pages 246 – 249. It is in the back section entitled, "A Complete System of Bible Studies." In addition, we will include a few other Old Covenant prophecies that describe the character and heart of God. Many of the New Covenant passages, especially those that involve actions and attitudes of Jesus, will also be considered.

o o o o o

Bailiff: *Please present the Introduction to the*

Prophecies of the Seed and Lineage of the Messiah

If we consider how many generations there were from the time of Eve to the time of Noah, followed by hundreds of years through Abraham, Isaac, Jacob, then Judah, the number of descendants would be staggering. Matthew begins with Abraham and lists the names of people who were part of the legacy of Jesus. The number of possibilities cannot be calculated by even the best computers of today, because there is no record of most of these descendants. Moses, who was guided by God's Spirit in writing the first five books of the Old Covenant, gave us many names to consider.

It seems the Messiah should have come through the tribe of Levi, the priestly tribe, but God's plan was for the Messiah to come through Judah! All this gives us reason to know that only God could determine this information. The prophets listed the names of Jesse and David, for example, not from their own knowledge; their information came from the guidance of God.

The Prophet is God, Himself

Prophecy: Genesis 3:15

After Eve was deceived by Satan in the form of a serpent, God put a curse on Satan and then said, speaking to Satan of the One to come:

And I will put enmity between you and the woman
and between your offspring and hers;
he will crush your head,
and you will strike his heel.

There are two parts to the fulfillment: the enmity between Satan and the woman and her seed, and the victory over Satan by the resurrection of Jesus. The fulfillment texts are found throughout the New Testament, but especially in the four Gospels.

The ones who cried out, "Crucify Him!" thought they would have no more problems from Jesus, but God knew that when He raised Jesus from the tomb, it would be a conquering of death, over which Satan ruled. By the resurrection, Jesus crushed the head of Satan. The crucifixion was just *striking the heel* compared to conquering death, *which Jesus came to do!*

The resurrection of the physical body of Jesus proved that life comes from Jesus, the Son of God. But even more important, this shows that Jesus offers a way to conquer evil in all its forms. We do not have the power or ability to overcome death; that is God's domain; but He has given us the responsibility to overcome evil, by His guidance, patience, mercy, and love.

The seed began with Eve, and thousands of years later, Mary gave birth to the Savior. The details of this birth are given in Matthew and Luke, but the fulfillment of this part of the prophecy is that Jesus was born as the seed of a woman.

The Messiah came, not as an angel or heavenly being, but as a human, with a human mother.

Again, the Prophet is God

In an earlier chapter we studied God's promise to Abraham. The fulfillment of the fourth part of God's promise was the birth, life, and sacrifice of Jesus for the sins of all the people of this world. The ones God chose to be in the bloodline to Jesus are also a part of this prophecy.

The prophecy in the promise to Abraham placed him in the genealogy of Jesus (Luke 3:23 – 38). The One promised to come was to fulfill every detail of that prophecy. Being a blessing to **all the people of the world** is impossible for **anyone other than Jesus** to fulfill.

History tells of many people who have made efforts to correct the wrongs of the world, whether political, religious, or social. Mahatma Ghandi became famous for his efforts to get rid of the stench of the caste system. Woodrow Wilson had a plan to engage all nations in a serious effort to live in peace with one another. Dr. Martin Luther King, Jr. had a dream that every person would be judged "**not by the color of his skin, but by the content of his character.**" The highly respected Dr. King spoke with the heart of Jesus, challenging all people to change the way they looked at others, to think and act with the heart of Jesus. However, none of these great people did what Jesus did – offer Himself for the sins of an evil world. None of these great men could pay the price for his own sins, much less the sins of all the people of the world.

Only by the plan God made to bring peace between Jew and Gentile – and that includes all the people of the world – would it be possible to have peace and salvation for everyone. God still expects each individual to make the choice not to do evil, but rather to listen to His words and *look for and walk* in His Light.

God clearly identifies the offspring of Abraham as the line through which all the nations of the earth will be blessed.

Prophecy: Genesis 17:19

Then God said, "Yes, but your wife
Sarah will bear you a son,
and you will call him Isaac. I will
establish my covenant with him
as an everlasting covenant for his
descendants after him.

Isaac is the son of the promise, but God made a choice between Isaac's twin sons. Esau, the first born by a few minutes, sold his birthright to his younger brother, Jacob, for a bowl of stew. In those times it was more than customary for the first-born son to inherit his father's estate. By selling his birthright to his younger brother, Esau broke that tradition, later regretting what he had done.

Prophecy: Genesis 28:14

This passage tells us the promise was continued through Jacob. Numbers 24:17 also reveals Jacob to be in the line from which the Messiah would come.

Your descendants will be like the dust of the earth,
and you will spread out to the west and to the east,
to the north and to the south. All peoples on earth
will be blessed through you and your offspring.

Remembering just a little world history, we know that the Jewish people did spread out to many parts of the world. But the seed was continued through Jacob. The specific words, **All peoples on earth will be blessed,** are directly from the promise God made to Abraham.

Prophecy: Genesis 49:10

The Patriarch, Jacob, had twelve sons, but only one could carry on the lineage to Jesus.

The scepter will not depart from Judah,
nor the ruler's staff from
between his feet, until he to whom it
belongs shall come and the
obedience of the nations shall be his.

Interesting! Judah was not the oldest son of Jacob and he was not from the priestly tribe of Levi. This does not follow Jewish priestly law, or family customs of inheritance, or the traditional way of earthly royalty; there seems to be a random selection from the descendants of Jacob. This break from so many traditions compels us to recognize that there is a higher power in charge, especially since these changes are clearly foretold in the scriptures.

There are no such daring prophecies
anywhere, by any religion,
that compares to the way God chose the
people for this lineage! (EBT)

By putting several passages together we can see how impossible it would be for any human being to foresee such an amazing projection of a lineage. God did not put anyone in this line who did not belong – **He made no mistakes and he kept predicting this lineage for a period of over 4000 years!**

Prophecy: Isaiah 9:7, 6

The Prophet Isaiah identified many details of the Messiah to come. He wrote his sixty-six chapters of prophecies more than 700 years before Jesus was born. Yet he stated that the lineage would go through David, who died nearly 300 years before Isaiah wrote. And, yes, David is a descendant of Abraham, Isaac, Jacob, and Judah. Here is what Isaiah wrote in his ninth chapter.

7 Of the greatness of his government and peace
there will be no end. He will reign on David's throne
and over his kingdom, establishing and upholding it
with justice and righteousness from
that time on and forever.
The zeal of the LORD Almighty will accomplish this.

Of whom was this spoken? The verse before verse 7 tells us clearly.

6 For to us a child is born, to us a son is given,
and the government will be on his shoulders.
And he will be called Wonderful Counselor,
Mighty God, Everlasting Father, Prince of Peace.

This is a very famous passage foretelling not only that the Messiah would come as a descendant of David, but also predicting the work He would do. The Messiah would come in human form, and would be a Son. Jesus fulfilled all of this precisely. The four terms, **Wonderful Counselor, Mighty God, Everlasting Father, Prince of Peace,** reveal more about the heart and character of the Messiah.

Prophecy: Isaiah 11:1

Isaiah presents another powerful description of the line from Abraham to Jesus.

A shoot will come up from the stump of Jesse;
from his roots a Branch will bear fruit.

Jesse was the father of David, Bethlehem was their home, and Jesus was born in Bethlehem. Matthew 1:1 – 17 details the lineage of Jesus back to Abraham; Luke 3:23 – 38 traces the lineage back to Adam.

o o o o o

Bailiff: *Please present your findings for:*

Prophecies that tell us of

The Birth and Early Childhood of Jesus

Prophecy: Micah 5:2

Micah stated that the one who would be the ruler in Israel would be born in the little town of Bethlehem. Even though it was not a large town, it was the hometown of David, as already mentioned.

> *But you, Bethlehem Ephrathah, though*
> *you are small among the clans*
> *of Judah, out of you will come for me*
> *one who will be ruler over*
> *Israel, whose origins are from of old, from ancient times.*

The birth of Jesus did not take place in Nazareth where Joseph and Mary lived, but in Bethlehem. Joseph and Mary had to go to their own home town for a census as ordered by Caesar Augustus. *Can you visualize Mary, heavy with a child soon to be born, probably riding on a donkey for that trip to Bethlehem – a trip of about 70 miles?*

Did Augustus decide *at that unusual time* to require taxes to be paid in everyone's hometown, or did God know that far ahead and cause the planning of Augustus to fit His own? It is foolish to even ask such questions. Or, can we realize the truth:

God put the whole plan together and made it work! Think about the details: the prophet stated that in Bethlehem a child would be born who would be the Christ, and that is where Jesus was born. This prophecy is specific as to the place of the Messiah's birth.

Micah also predicted that this child would grow up to be *the ruler over Israel.* What kind of Kingdom of Israel would this be? A physical, political entity? Or something else entirely? When they took Jesus to the palace, Pilate came out to hear the charges against Him, and the Jewish leaders poured out their vehement accusations. Pilate went back into his palace and asked Jesus in a straightforward manner, *Are you the King of the Jews?* The answer Jesus gave did not disturb Pilate, as a different answer might have. The Lord simply made an unthreatening statement to Pilate.

John 18:36 – 37

36 Jesus said, "My kingdom is not
of this world. If it were,
my servants would fight to prevent my
arrest by the Jewish leaders.
But now my kingdom is from another place."

37 "You are a king, then!" said Pilate.
Jesus answered, "You say that I am a king.
In fact, the reason I was born and came into the world
is to testify to the truth.
Everyone on the side of truth listens to me."

Convinced that Jesus posed no problem for himself or his rule, Pilate went back to the Jewish leaders and said, *I find no basis for a charge against him* (v. 38). Pilate recognized that Jesus did claim a kingdom, but not one to threaten his sovereignty. *But those leaders did not hear the conversation between Pilate and Jesus.*

Who knows how many miracles Jesus had performed before the eyes of the Jewish people, including many of their leaders? They should have known that this man from Nazareth was doing things only God could do. Their thinking was that the main task of the Messiah would be to drive the Romans back to Rome. With this idea so entrenched in their minds, they could no longer comprehend the message of the Messianic prophets.

It is in the hearts of all people, Jew and Gentile, that Jesus came to be the ruler. This failure to understand these great prophets resulted in the crucifixion of Jesus. We need to come to grips with another aspect of that misunderstanding.

What does the word "Israel" mean? First, it is the name God gave to Jacob by which all his descendants would be called, *the Children of Israel.* However, there is a very important differentiation to be recognized. From God's viewpoint, being a physical descendant of Jacob does not make one an Israelite. God's purpose for His "Israel" – not the physical descendants of Abraham – is explained by Paul in Romans.

Romans 9:8

In other words, it is not the natural
children who are God's children,
but it is the children of the promise who are regarded
as Abraham's offspring.

Paul states it another way in his letter to the believers in Galatia by calling them the *Israel of God* (Galatians 6:16). There are a number of things that help us understand what the Lord has in mind for this *Israel of God,* which is more than the people in the bloodline from Abraham. It is basically referring to all those included in the promise that God would bless all people, Jew and Gentile, through the One, the Messiah, whom God would send.

Only God could fulfill so many specific prophecies! These great prophets spoke words which strengthen our belief **that God is the author of it all**. Only God is able to know and record centuries in advance, and in such great detail, the lineage from Adam through Abraham to Jesus. Thinking about *the awesome foreknowledge of God* brings us to our knees in humble praise.

The story of Joseph and Mary in Bethlehem where Jesus was born is so famous, it is not necessary to tell it again. Here is a similar prophecy.

Prophecy: Isaiah 7:14

*Therefore the Lord himself will give
you a sign: The virgin will
conceive and give birth to a son,
and will call him Immanuel.*

Scholars may argue about the meaning of "virgin" in this verse, but Luke makes it clear. When the angel, Gabriel, spoke to Mary and told her that she had found favor with God, she was greatly troubled. Gabriel also told her that she would give birth to a son. Mary was astonished and asked the angel a question.

Luke 1:34b

How will this be since I am a virgin?

Mary was engaged to marry Joseph, but the marriage had not yet been consummated. When Joseph learned that Mary was pregnant, he considered putting her away, as Jewish custom demanded. Why not? What changed his mind? Matthew explains it step by step.

Matthew 1:18 – 25

*18 This is how the birth of Jesus
the Messiah came about:
His mother Mary was pledged to be married to Joseph,
but before they came together, she was found
to be pregnant through the Holy Spirit.*

*19 Because Joseph her husband was faithful to the law,
and yet did not want to expose her to public disgrace,
he had in mind to divorce her quietly.*

*20 But after he had considered this, an angel of the Lord
appeared to him in a dream and
said, "Joseph son of David,
do not be afraid to take Mary home as your wife,
because what is conceived in her is from the Holy Spirit.
21 She will give birth to a son, and you
are to give him the name Jesus,
because he will save his people from their sins."*

*22 All this took place to fulfill what the Lord had said
through the prophet: 23 "The virgin will conceive and
give birth to a son, and they will call him Immanuel"
(which means "God with us").*

*24 When Joseph woke up, he did
what the angel of the Lord
had commanded him and took Mary home as his wife.*

*25 But he did not consummate their marriage
until she gave birth to a son. And he
gave him the name Jesus.*

Mary first, then Joseph, believed the words of Gabriel. They waited until after the birth of Jesus to consummate their marriage. The evidence that Mary had never known a man is quite reasonable, even strong. Joseph did not put Mary away, contrary to Jewish culture. This gives credibility to Joseph's belief in and obedience to the angel's words.

Prophecy: Jeremiah 31:15

Jeremiah prophesied the massacre of children, confirmed by Matthew. This is the first of many atrocious attempts to harm Jesus, beginning just after His birth!

This is what the LORD says: "A voice is heard in Ramah, mourning and great weeping, Rachel weeping for her children and refusing to be comforted, because they are no more."

Matthew quotes the complete prophecy of Jeremiah, a good example of how sincere the Jewish people were in their belief in a Messiah to come. They knew the prophecy and later realized its fulfillment. How did Jesus escape this massacre?

When Herod realized that the Magi had deceived him, he was extremely angry, and ordered that all boys in Bethlehem, two years old and under, be killed. Matthew tells us that Jeremiah had prophesied that slaughter (Jeremiah 31:15), and quotes Jeremiah.

Matthew 2:18

"A voice is heard in Ramah, weeping and great mourning, Rachel weeping for her children and refusing to be comforted, because they are no more."

God knew how angry Herod would be after being deceived by the Magi, and executed His plan to protect Jesus and his parents. After the Magi left Joseph, Mary, and the infant Jesus, an angel of the Lord appeared to Joseph in a dream and told him to get up and take his family to Egypt. He did, and stayed there until after Herod died. An angel again appeared to Joseph and told him to return to the land of Israel. He did, but when he learned that Archelaus, the son of Herod, was reigning in the place of his father, he took Mary and Jesus north to Nazareth in Galilee (Matthew 2:13 – 23). What did Hosea, the prophet, say would happen? He prophesied that this child, a son, would be called out of Egypt. (Hosea 11:1). We see again that a New Testament writer knew what the prophet said, and saw the direct fulfillment of it.

There is another event in the childhood of Jesus for which there is no direct prophecy, but there is a prophecy containing the essence of what took place. In Isaiah 11, verses 2 – 4, he describes characteristics of a full-grown, very mature person.

He will have **The Spirit of wisdom and of understanding, of counsel and of might,** and **The Spirit of the knowledge and fear of the LORD.** His judgment will not be with His eyes or ears, but with **righteousness for the poor and needy.** He will not use weapons of physical warfare to slay his enemies, but will use **the rod of his mouth.** Paul discussed this in 2 Thessalonians 2:8 when he wrote that Jesus would overthrow the **lawless one with the breath of His mouth.** Verse 1 of that chapter mentions **the stump of Jesse,** obviously referring to Jesus.

This brings us to Luke 2:41 – 52, an event involving Jesus at age twelve. Every year Joseph and Mary took Jesus to Jerusalem to the festival of the Passover. On this occasion everything was usual except when they left to return to Nazareth. Jesus was not with His parents. They were not concerned for they thought He was with His friends, children of other families on the road. However, when they stopped for the night, they could not find him. They returned to Jerusalem and searched for three days – finally finding him in the temple courts. What was this twelve-year-old boy doing in the temple courts?

He was *sitting among the teachers, listening to them and asking them questions!* (v. 46). How did these teachers and all the others present react to this young lad? They were *amazed at his understanding and his answers* (v. 47). How does this compare to the very mature adult characteristics found in Isaiah 11:2 – 4?

The characteristics of the Messiah as given by Isaiah are usually thought of as being those of an adult. The *Spirit of wisdom and of understanding* is not considered normal for a twelve-year-old boy, but what happened in the temple reveals the uniqueness of Jesus at that age.

We may not consider the prophecy of Isaiah 11 to apply to the Messiah as a child, but Luke causes us to reconsider. The adult teachers were amazed at the understanding and answers the twelve-year-old Jesus gave them, and they saw the evident depth of His understandings.

From this account, we should realize that Jesus was not the ordinary son of a carpenter. He did not dispute with these adult leaders or accuse them of anything wrong. They did not show any resentment to this young lad. As they were amazed at His questions and understandings, so should we be.

. . . And Jesus grew in wisdom and stature, and in favor with God and man . . .

Luke 2:52

CHAPTER NINE

The Messiah and His Ministry

Me: *Your Honor, there are many aspects
of the ministry of Jesus,
and often there are several in the same passage. I will
try to identify the more relevant ones.*
Judge: *Very well. You may make your presentations.*
Me: *Thank you, your Honor.*

Bailiff: *Please present your findings for*

Prophecies of the Ministry of Jesus

Perhaps we often think of the ministry of Jesus as basically His call for all people to repent and come to Him for salvation. There is no question about that part of His ministry being an absolute necessity for us. However, *we may miss the mark, and not even hit the target at all*, if we do not pay close attention to the **whole ministry of Jesus**.

Some of the things Jesus did cannot be done by anyone today: walking on the water, calling for the winds and waves to become calm, raising Lazarus from the tomb after four days, and many more. But if we pay attention to His heart, His love, His compassion, His mercy, His grace, and His forgiveness, we can learn what God wants us to become.

The Prophet Is Isaiah

Isaiah tells of some terrible things that happened to the northern tribes of Israel in chapter 8, but concludes in the beginning of chapter 9 with words about the land of Galilee where Jesus began His ministry. He predicts that the Galileans, who formerly walked in darkness, will see a great light. Matthew recognizes this prophecy and quotes much of it.

Matthew 4:12 – 16

12 When Jesus heard that John had been put in prison, he withdrew to Galilee. 13 Leaving Nazareth, he went and lived in Capernaum, which was by the lake in the area of Zebulun and Naphtali— 14 to fulfill what was said through the prophet Isaiah:

15 "Land of Zebulun and land of Naphtali, the Way of the Sea, beyond the Jordan, Galilee of the Gentiles—

16 the people living in darkness have seen a great light; on those living in the land of the shadow of death a light has dawned."

Jesus was the Light that was dawning in Galilee. John records a brief trip that Jesus made to Jerusalem for Passover performing miraculous signs (John 2:23 – 24). However, the Pharisees took notice that Jesus' disciples were immersing more disciples than John. It is possible that this is when the Pharisees began to look on Jesus as a threat, and could be the reason Jesus decided to return to Galilee (John 4:1 – 3).

Jesus wants to transform us into His **children of light.** We are to reflect His light for the very purpose of dispelling the darkness that engulfs our sinful world. Do not forget that God had in His mind the reconciliation of Jew and Gentile. He began His ministry **beyond the Jordan, Galilee of the Gentiles.** We know that both John the Immerser and Jesus the Christ began their ministries by calling for the people to **Repent, for the Kingdom of God is near** (Matthew 3:1 – 3; 4:17).

> **Me: Your Honor, these many passages all apply**
> **to understanding the heart of God and the Messiah.**
> **May I present them without interruption which**
> **might distract the attention of the readers?**
> **Judge: Yes, you may.**
> **Me: Thank you, Your honor.**

The Prophet is Isaiah

Isaiah had many concepts of the true Messiah to proclaim to the Jewish nation. In his fifty-third chapter, Isaiah wrote eloquently of the Messiah, and in verse 4, he opened up an avenue of thinking about Jesus as the Suffering Savior.

Isaiah 53:4

Surely he took up our pain and bore our suffering,
yet we considered him punished by God,
stricken by him, and afflicted.

How did Jesus **take up our pain and bear our suffering?** Jesus, the **Word that became flesh** and lived among us, did many things for people that revealed His perfect love. He had love for all kinds of people: lepers, blind, deaf, crippled, hungry, even the unknowing. If we limit His ministry to what He taught, we vaguely see a loving Savior. How Jesus taught us by His words is important; how Jesus taught us by His example is the key to life. The way His actions blended with His own heart and teachings is awesome. He put His whole being into doing the Father's will, *so that we could be saved from sin.* It is much easier to accept His teachings when we see how He put **whole-hearted love** into bringing salvation to all people.

Many New Testament passages reveal the caring heart of Jesus during His ministry. Most of these events took place in Galilee. In addition to teaching, a very important part of the ministry of Jesus focused on: helping and comforting the people, giving sight to the blind, healing the lepers, restoring hearing for the deaf and speech to the mute, even raising the dead. (See also Isaiah 35.)

After moving from Nazareth to Capernaum, by the Sea of Galilee in the region of Zebulun and Naphtali, Jesus began to call for men to follow Him and become His disciples.

He was in Galilee, so of course large crowds from Galilee followed Him; many others came from the Decapolis area and the region across the Jordan, as well as from Jerusalem and Judea. There is no doubt but that word of these miraculous healing events became known very quickly from Judea to northern Galilee and on into Syria, and from east of the Jordan to the Mediterranean Sea (Matthew 4:23 – 25).

To focus on the teaching and preaching of Jesus, and fail to pay careful attention to His whole ministry, is a certain way to miss the mark. Remember, a definition for *sin* is to *miss the mark!*

In general, what does a minister do? A minister is one who has a mission to perform, and he goes about carrying out that mission. With Jesus, it is difficult to write about His "ministry" and not include the heart, mind, soul, and character of Jesus that motivated His every action. The compassion of Jesus is seen in healing the sick; we really need to have the deep Christ-like love for all suffering people.

Many of those who appealed to Jesus for healing, for themselves or for others, had a faith of their own. We wonder how those people came to that much faith, that they could ask Jesus to heal someone who was not present.

We need to see the whole of the heart of Jesus and, if possible, to see the effect it had on all who were witnesses of these miracles. When we realize the truth of their faith, will not our faith also be strengthened?

After going up a mountain in Galilee and delivering what we call the *Sermon on the Mount,* Jesus found large crowds following Him, among them a leper. The leper said to Jesus, **"Lord, if you are willing, you can make me clean."** (Matthew 8:2b).

It was not a question of, **Could** *Jesus heal him of leprosy?* This was the question, **Was Jesus willing** *to heal him?* The leper seemed **to know** that Jesus **could heal him**! Jesus reached out His hand and touched the man *(No one ever touched a leper!)* and replied, *I am willing.* **Be clean** (v. 3b). **Jesus touched and healed this leper!** Why? He saw a need and He did what God gave Him the power to do.

Did He see, with His eyes alone, what the leper needed, or did He also see with His loving heart? How do we see our part in the ministry of Jesus? Can we see ourselves serving as the kind of ministers Jesus wants us to be? Incidentally, Jesus wants all of us to be changed into *His ministers.* The role of ministers in many different churches today varies as much as the changing directions of the winds that blow. That is why we need to clearly understand two things: One, what did Jesus come to do; what **was** His ministry? Two, what is **our part** in His ministry? Keep these two questions in mind any time you study anything about Jesus and His ministry.

The next event is about a Roman centurion who knew about Jesus. His faith is quite unusual. This story comes from Matthew 8 (Also see Luke 7:2 – 10).

The centurion, probably the head of the Roman forces in Capernaum, came to Jesus and asked for help on behalf of one of his servants who was paralyzed and was suffering greatly. Jesus replied by asking if the centurion wanted Him to go to the servant and heal him. We do not know how this centurion came to such faith, but the reply he gave Jesus reveals an unusually strong belief. He explained that although he also was a man with great authority, he did not feel worthy for Jesus to go to his home. He said to Jesus, *"But just say the word, and my servant will be healed."* (v. 8b).

The plea of the centurion reveals several things. First, he had heard about Jesus and was convinced that Jesus could heal his servant. Second, the centurion had a heart of compassion for his servant. And third, he believed that Jesus did not need to go to his home, but He needed to just *say the word, and my servant will be healed.* The confidence of this centurion in the power of Jesus *borders almost on knowledge!*

Perhaps the centurion realized that Jesus had authority even greater than his own. He believed all Jesus had to do was to *say the word,* and his servant would be healed. This centurion, a very humble man, realized his servant was deathly ill. He had compassion on him, and wanted Jesus to make him well.

Can we as Christians realize that perpetrators of gross evil are deathly ill? Jesus came to save all the lost, even the evil-doers! Have we set our hearts to be in tune with the heart of Jesus? Do we think of evil-doers as being deathly ill and in great need of a healer? Do we take actions to introduce them to *the Healer, Jesus?* Or is our desire for vengeance greater than our love for God? The centurion's faith in Jesus as a healer spurred him to action.

Under the leadership of Jesus, we are given the responsibility to lead sinners out of sin. What kind of sin are we talking about? From God's viewpoint, are there "big" sins and "little" sins? From our human viewpoint, we may overlook what we individually consider a "little" sin *in ourselves*, and be horrified by someone else committing a "big" sin. Jesus did not come just for committers of "big" sins; He came for all of us who commit sins of any kind. There is a problem: all of us have difficulty following the leadership of Jesus – He wants all sinners saved – and we are to be His instruments, His ministers to **all** those lost in sin.

However, it is still difficult to love the perpetrators of gross evil and want them to be saved. It is a normal human response to want them to be punished. The shame and agony Jesus suffered on the cross *to save all sinners,* which includes "perpetrators of evil," should shake us out of our desire for vengeance. From His heart Jesus prayed to God for His murderers to be forgiven! The loving, forgiving heart of Jesus calls us to tell the lost there is hope, tell them to come to **the Healer of souls, Jesus** – *and tell them so with a heart **that cares enough to want them healed.***

Just as the centurion cared for his servant and took determined action, so must we care for sinners *and determine* to bring them to Jesus. The True Healer saw great faith in the Roman soldier's heart. Jesus recognized and praised the faith of the centurion; w*hat kind of faith does Jesus recognize in me?*

When Jesus heard the plea of the centurion and his request for Jesus to just **say the word**, He was amazed. He said that He had not found such strong faith in the whole land of Israel!. Furthermore, he said there would be **weeping and gnashing of teeth** by the **subjects of the kingdom** because they would be **thrown outside** (v. 11, 12).

Why will **the subjects of the kingdom** be **thrown outside**? The only logical answer is they were subjects of the kingdom, but did not remain faithful to the King! What about us today? Is the first level of our faith permanent, or must we intentionally keep it growing as long as we live? Now, what happened to the servant?

Then Jesus said to the centurion,
"Go! Let it be done just as you
believed it would." And his servant was
healed at that moment (Matthew 8:13).

Jesus healed the centurion's servant who was too sick to be carried to Jesus. He did it by declaring, **Let it be done just as you believed it would.** Jesus praised the centurion's faith proclaiming, **Truly I tell you, I have not found anyone in Israel with such great faith** (v. 10).

In this same chapter of Matthew, there are two other important events: the healing of Peter's mother-in-law, and the exorcism of many evil spirits (8:14 – 17).

Jesus simply touched the hand of Peter's mother-in-law, and the fever left her so quickly that she got up and waited on Him. She prepared food or drink, whatever was needed for Him. That evening, Jesus spoke His words and the evil spirits were driven out of the demon-possessed. Jesus healed all the others who were sick. Notice that the text says Jesus healed **ALL THE SICK.** Note: not one word about Jesus preaching or teaching was recorded. The ministry of Jesus included teaching, of course, but compassionate actions were also a vital part of His ministry.

Matthew credits these actions of Jesus as a fulfillment of Isaiah 53:4, quoting these words, **"He took up our infirmities and bore our diseases"** (v. 17b). Reading these passages helps us to know the very heart of Jesus as He lived day-by-day. *That is the kind of heart Jesus wants to develop in all of us.*

Matthew 8:25 – 27 is another passage that fulfills Isaiah 53:4. Jesus was with His disciples on the Sea of Galilee when a very strong windstorm threatened to sink the boat. They were frightened (Jesus was asleep). In their fear they woke Jesus, shouting to him, **Lord, save us! We are going to drown!** (v. 25). The reply of Jesus was a rebuke, not for waking him up, but because of their "**little faith.**" He then asked them, **"Why** *are you so afraid?"* (v. 26). Matthew used a term translated as "rebuked" in the NIV to describe how Jesus calmed both the winds and the waves. His disciples in the boat were dumbfounded, and asked, probably among themselves, *"What kind of man is this? Even the winds and the waves obey him!"* (v. 27).

By healing all kinds of sicknesses, Jesus demonstrated His power over our physical bodies. When He rebuked the winds and the waves, and when He walked on the turbulent waters of the Sea of Galilee, He demonstrated His power and control over the natural laws. Matthew, an eye-witness as were the other disciples in the boat, recorded both of these events.

What these disciples saw bewildered them, overpowered them. It brought them beyond the level of just "believing" Jesus; the evidence of what He did *helped them* **know** *that Jesus came from God.* **What kind of man is this? Even the winds and the waves obey him!** The question was not about what they saw Jesus do. They were astonished that the winds and waves obeyed Him. A short time after this incident, they saw Jesus walking on the rough sea waters, and thought He was a ghost. They saw Peter sinking beneath the waves, and they saw Jesus, *standing on the sea,* pulling him up to safety! (Matthew 14:22 – 33). Do you think these events strengthened the faith of His disciples? Do they strengthen our faith?

There is one more event in Matthew, chapter 8, that relates to the prophecy in Isaiah 53:4. It tells how Jesus healed two demon-possessed men, freeing them from their misery. We will also learn more details from Mark's account in chapter 5.

The account of these two demon-possessed men (Mark mentions only one) reveals several surprising facts. One, the demons in these men recognized Jesus as the Son of God (v. 29). Two, they knew their time of punishment for their evil lives was yet in the future. Three, they acknowledged that Jesus had the power to command them to leave the two men and be sent wherever He wished (v. 31). We may wonder why they begged

Jesus to send them into a nearby herd of pigs, but they did; and Jesus simply said *Go!* – and the demons entered the herd of pigs. The whole herd ran down the slope into the lake and drowned (v. 32).

In Mark's account, this very strong man told Jesus that his name was Legion. In the military terms of those days, it meant an army of three to four thousand, but in general usage, it means a great number. Therefore it is reasonable to say that the man who was possessed by these demons is referring to the countless number of demons inside him. In Mark 5:12, it is the demons that are begging Jesus, not the man possessed by them. Therefore, it is the demons that are legion in number. Mark also states that the herd of pigs was *about two thousand in number* (v. 13). The entire herd plunged into the sea. The herdsmen who saw this went into their village and reported all to the townspeople.

Jesus used His power to exorcise the demons from the two men and redirect them into the pigs. There were too many witnesses of this event to call it into question: all the disciples and others with Jesus, and the herdsmen who reported to the village.

How many of the villagers went out to see the drowned pigs? Were some dead pigs still floating in the lake? What caused the villagers to urge Jesus and His disciples to leave? Were the people glad to see two healed, normal men; or were they angry with Jesus who had destroyed their huge herd? They did not even recognize the hand of God in what Jesus had done! Such powerful evidence should have made the Gadarene people ask questions – Who is this Jesus that can calm so violent a man? (Mark 5:3, 4) – *but they did not, they just wanted Jesus to leave!* (v. 17; Matthew 8:34).

Many other events from the Gospels also fulfill Isaiah 53:4. These selections from Mark, Luke, and John will also enhance our understanding of how Jesus fulfilled this prophecy. Our understanding of the heart and soul of Jesus is deepened as we see how He ministered day by day. Do we think of our own ministry as a daily opportunity to demonstrate the compassion and love of Jesus?

Jesus had left the region of Tyre and returned to the region of the Decapolis, east of the Sea of Galilee, where this next event occurred (Mark 7:32 – 37). Some people brought a deaf man, who had much trouble speaking, to Jesus. They begged Him to **place his hand on him.** Jesus quietly took him away from the crowd before taking action. He put His fingers into the man's ears, and cried out *"Be opened!"* (v. 34). Not only was he able to hear, he could **speak plainly** (v. 35). Jesus told the people, who brought the deaf man, not to tell anyone, but did they tell?

This brings up a question about what Jesus commanded these people **not** to do. Everyone knew the man was deaf and his speech was garbled, and here he is *speaking plainly and able to hear clearly.* How could anyone not ask about what had happened? How could the healed man not tell anyone about Jesus? Jesus certainly knew what had to happen and in His heart was happy for the man. Jesus knew that some things just had to be told, and *thanking God and Jesus for the many blessings They give* **is what we all must do!**

What did putting his fingers into the man's ears, then spitting and touching the man's tongue, have to do with the healing? The important thing is to understand that Jesus had full control over the nerves that send sound to the brain, and over the nerves that send speech to the voice box, enabling the man to hear and to speak **clearly!**

Is there any teaching, example, or command for the disciples of Jesus to go about healing all sick people in or out of hospitals? However, we believe that Jesus expects us to have His caring and compassionate heart for the sick, do what we are able to do, and pray for God to do what He has not enabled us to do. Sometimes, perhaps, all God expects us to do is say

129

a kind word to a stranger, or pray with a person who knows it is about time to go into eternity with God.

The next passage from Luke 7:11 – 16, helps us know that God gave Jesus the power over life and death, even before He conquered death by way of the cross. He went with His disciples to Nain and a large crowd went with Him. As they arrived at the town gate, Jesus saw bearers carrying out the body of the only son of a widow, and many of her friends from the town were with her. Seeing this touched the heart of Jesus and He said to her, *"Don't cry"* (v. 13). He then went up to the bier, causing the bearers to stand still. To the body on the bier, Jesus said, *"Young man, I say to you, get up!"* (v. 14). In response, the young man sat up and began to speak. Jesus then brought the mother and son together. Needless to say, their friends were astonished, but notice what they did in response: they praised God. They also said two things: *"A great prophet has appeared among us,"* and, *"God has come to help his people"* (v. 16). They saw that what Jesus did was from God and praised Him.

In the account of the deaf man, the people just had to tell what happened, *Jesus could make the deaf to hear and the dumb to speak!* But the Gadarenes did not think or ask, "Who made it possible for this demon-possessed man to now be in his right mind?" The Gadarenes were **also** people Jesus came to save.

It takes deliberate action of both mind and heart to see what other people need: a smile, a prayer, a gentle touch that says *I am here for you, what can I do to help?* That is the mark of one living with the heart of Jesus.

How many of us would die for someone else, even a loved one, as Jesus gave Himself for us? The sacrifice that Jesus made *for us* came *when we were powerless, ungodly, still sinners, and enemies of God Himself.* That is who **we were** when Jesus came! (Romans 5:6 – 11).

When we focus only on ourselves, it is difficult to recognize the needs of others. Jesus wants us *to see those needs.* It is obvious that **His heart was full of concern, love, and compassion for all those He healed!** It is clear that Jesus had compassion on the dead young man, but **the actions of Jesus *began* with His heartfelt compassion for the mother.**

Please, Father, open our eyes to see both the physical and the spiritual needs of those around us. In Jesus' Name!

CHAPTER TEN

Understanding the Compassion of Jesus

All four of the Gospel writers tell of the miracle of the feeding of the 5000. Both Matthew and Mark state the heart of the ministry of Jesus clearly.

Matthew 14:14

When Jesus landed and saw a large crowd, he had compassion on them and healed their sick.

Mark 6:34

*When Jesus landed and saw a large
crowd, he had compassion
on them, because they were like
sheep without a shepherd.
So he began teaching them many things.*

Jesus had compassion on them, healed their sick, and taught them the truth. What Jesus did reveals that He not only had compassion on them, but did something about it. He performed a miracle of feeding 5000 men (Matthew stated

besides the women and children) with a few loaves of barley bread and a few fish!

Feeding the hungry and healing the sick are important. But Jesus knew that people needed something even more important; they needed to be taught about the **True and Living God.** Do we have the correct balance in our compassion for those lost in addictive sin? Jesus blessed all the sick with healing, and He blessed all people by teaching them the truth. However, each one had to decide whether or not to accept that truth, *and live by it.*

Jesus both fed the hungry crowd and taught them the truth. How can we follow Jesus in a similar way today? Here are some examples.

English is being taught by devoted Christians to people who have no knowledge of Jesus. The word of God is used as a reading text, resulting in thousands being led to Christ.

Wells are being dug to provide clean water for people in need, but the spiritual teachings of Jesus accompany that good work.

In the U.S., when disaster strikes – storms, floods, fires, or other tragedies – truckloads of food, clothing, and other necessities are *already prepared for shipment.* Truck drivers haul these urgently needed loads to local congregations in the disaster areas. Caring Christians distribute items to those suffering great loss.

Poor Christian families in rural areas overseas are given a pregnant female animal, whether pig, goat, or cow. The family agrees to raise that animal, and in time, to give a female offspring to another needy family, and the process continues. Local Christians oversee this and share the love and teachings of Jesus.

These are examples of the ministry of Jesus that many *willing-to-help* Christians can do today. There are more similar good works that combine compassionate care with teaching the gospel. God wants His children of light to be doing the good works that He has prepared, *in advance,* for us to do. Let us read the text, then let it challenge us all to do more.

Ephesians 2:10

For we are God's handiwork, created in Christ Jesus to do good works, which God prepared in advance for us to do.

God sent Jesus to this earth to carry out many tasks: call people to repent, train disciples, perform miracles that no one could do unless God was with Him, teach everyone the Truth of God, expose hypocrisy, and offer Himself as a sacrifice for the sins we have all committed.

This ministry of Jesus included forgiving those who accused and crucified Him, the True Messiah. We are not called to be crucified, but we **are called** to be *living* sacrifices (Romans 12:1). That calling has no time limitations; we are to be *living sacrifices* all day every day.

The next example of the heart of Jesus comes from John 11. A man named Lazarus lived in Bethany with his two sisters, Mary and Martha. When Lazarus became very ill, his sisters sent word to Jesus, saying, *"Lord, the one you love is sick"* (v. 3). Jesus' response was unusual: *"This sickness will not end in death. No, it is for God's glory . . . "* (v. 4). *Now Jesus loved Martha and her sister and Lazarus* (v. 5). Surprisingly, He stayed where He was two more days (v. 6) before suggesting to His disciples, *"Let us go back to Judea"* (v. 7). On hearing this, the disciples became uneasy because just a short time before this the Jews there had tried to stone Him to death. They did not understand what Jesus' intentions were. Then He told them *"Our friend Lazarus has fallen asleep; but I am going there to wake him up"* (v. 11). Thinking He meant natural sleep, they took that as a good sign. *Then he told them* plainly, *"Lazarus is dead, and for your sake I am glad I was not there, so that you may believe"* (v. 14 – 15a).

When they arrived in Bethany, Jesus learned that *Lazarus had already been in the tomb for four days* (v. 17). Many friends from Jerusalem had made the two-mile journey to Bethany to comfort the family in their bereavement. Martha was told that *Jesus was coming, so she want out to meet Him, but Mary stayed at home* (v. 20).

Martha's first words to Jesus sounded like a reproach, but her next words demonstrated that her faith in Jesus was true. *"Lord," Martha said to Jesus, "if you had been here, my brother would not have died. But I know that even now God will give you whatever you ask"* (v. 21, 22). When Jesus assured Martha that her brother would rise again, she answered: *"I know he will rise again in the resurrection at the last day"* (v. 24).

How could she say *"I know"?* We do not know how Martha's faith became so strong, but it did. Jesus and His disciples had visited that home many times; Martha had many opportunities to hear Him speak and to hear the disciples recount their experiences with Jesus. The lesson for us to learn is: **the more** we *Keep our eyes fixed on Jesus* – **the more** we learn from Jesus – the **stronger our faith will become.** *May God help us encourage this truth to fill our hearts!*

Jesus' next words to Martha have become more than a mantra or a catch-phrase for Christians. They are the bedrock on which our life is based. Jesus said:

> *25 . . . "I am the resurrection and the life.*
> *The one who believes in me will*
> *live, even though they die;*
> *26 and whoever lives by believing*
> *in me will never die. . . ."*

136

When He asked Martha if she believed this, her answer was strong:

> **She said to Him, "Yes, Lord, I believe**
> **that You are the Christ,**
> **the Son of God, who is to come into the world."** (v. 27).

After this conversation, Martha went back and **called her sister Mary aside. "The Teacher is here . . . asking for you"** (v. 28). Mary immediately went to see Jesus who had not yet gone into the village. Some of the friends who had been with Mary noticed how quickly she left the house and followed her, thinking she was going out to the tomb to grieve.

When she saw Jesus, she fell at His feet and said the same thing her sister had said: **"Lord, if you had been here, my brother would not have died"** (v. 32). She was crying; the Jews who had come with her were crying; Jesus was **deeply moved in spirit and troubled** (v. 33). And then **Jesus wept** (v. 35).

Jesus experienced all the feelings we human beings have. He saw Mary and all her friends weeping, and He also wept. The mourning of those who had come from their homes, probably many from Jerusalem, was also one of genuine love for this family. We could ask questions about why Jesus wept, but the context is clear; His heart was in tune with the family of Lazarus, and with those who had come to comfort them.

The people there recognized how deeply Jesus had loved Lazarus. Some of them, who obviously knew of miraculous things Jesus had done, questioned, **"Could not he who opened the eyes of the blind man have kept this man from dying?"** (v. 37). Standing at the tomb, Jesus, surprising everyone there, commanded that the stone be rolled away from the entrance.

It was Martha who voiced the misgivings of all the crowd when she cautioned Jesus by saying, **"By this time there is a bad odor, for he has been there four days"** (v. 39). No one wanted to add such an unbearable horror to the grief already weighing them down. But then Jesus reminded her, *"Did I not tell you that if you believe, you will see the glory of God?"* (v. 40).

So the stone was rolled away; Jesus looked up to heaven and prayed: . . . *"Father, I thank you that you have heard me. I knew that you always hear me, but I said this for the benefit of the people standing here, that they may believe that you sent me"* (v. 41b, 42).

Then in a loud voice Jesus shouted, *"Lazarus, come out!* (v. 43). The dead man came out, strips of linen still binding his live body, as they had bound his dead body. *Perhaps, just a few days earlier. some of the friends of the family had helped wrap the body in grave clothes.* Jesus said, *"Let him go"* (v. 44). There was no question in the minds of all who were there. **Jesus had raised a dead body to life again, after four days in the tomb!** *They knew that God was with Jesus. They were witnesses of God's glory working through Jesus.*

This loving, amazing event brought faith to those who witnessed Lazarus, still wrapped in grave clothes, obeying the call of Jesus to come out of the tomb.

Many of the Jews who had come to comfort Lazarus' family saw what Jesus did and believed in Him. *But some of them* went to tell the Pharisees in Jerusalem. Did they go to share the good news, or were they just being loyal to the Pharisees? Actually, it does not matter; a reporter's responsibility is to be sure the news is true. Those who hear the report are responsible for what they do with it. So, how did the Pharisees and the chief priests respond to this astonishing news?

On hearing the report of Jesus raising Lazarus, the chief priests and the Pharisees called a meeting of the Sanhedrin, the official ruling body of the Jews. In the discussion that followed, they admitted that Jesus was performing many miraculous signs! What was their fear? Why were they not rejoicing that Lazarus was now alive? Would acknowledging that God was with Jesus in the raising of Lazarus be admitting that Jesus is the Messiah? Were they not all looking for the Messiah? The prophets had been predicting His coming for centuries!

The Jewish leaders considered the Messiah to be the one to lead a military force (like David?) and drive the Romans back to Rome. Were they totally oblivious of the military power of the Romans, or did they just ignore it? Failure to face reality is often a serious mistake, and sometimes fatal, as we learned from the prophecy of Moses (Deuteronomy 28). *None are so blind as those who will not see!*

Caiaphas, the High Priest for that year, had something to say which turned out to be a prophecy, but not for the reason he had in mind. He told the Jewish leaders, ***"It is better for you that one man die for the people than that the whole nation perish"*** (v. 50).

Caiaphas may have thought that crucifying Jesus would keep the Romans from causing trouble, but he just did not know. John enlarged on the idea the high priest was unknowingly prophesying. Jesus would die, *not only* for the Jewish nation, *but also* for the **scattered children of God, to bring them together and make them one** (v. 51, 52). This is very close to Paul's message in Ephesians 2:11 – 18, where he tells of God's plan to bring all people together as one in Christ Jesus. But the Sanhedrin, chief priests, and Pharisees had already reached a decision. For them, the only solution to the "Jesus problem" was to deliberately find a way to kill him.

From that day on, the Sanhedrin plotted to take the life of Jesus, and He no longer moved freely among the people of Judea. Jesus and His disciples left the area and went to a village called Ephraim, near a desert. The Jewish leaders could not find or arrest Him; that could happen only at the time God had determined. Jesus knew the Pharisees had Him on their "most wanted" list. The order had been given for His arrest. Their minds were closed; they had no other thought – *nail Him to a cross.*

CHAPTER ELEVEN

The Heart of God as Revealed in the Proverbs

BAILIFF: *Present your findings from the*

Proverbs of Solomon

Human character is revealed by what a person does, whether wise or unwise, good or evil, right or wrong. Solomon wrote many proverbs that reveal the heart of God, the way God expects us to behave. For example, in Proverbs 1:2 – 3, several words describe human behavior: ***wisdom, understanding, discipline, doing what is right, just, and fair.***

Understanding ***In the beginning was the word, and the word was with God, and the word was God . . . and the word became flesh and lived among us*** (John 1:1, 14) helps us know these characteristics are the heart nature of God. This study from the Proverbs will help us grasp what we need to be changed into. Every word or phrase we study will be like a low cloud that brings a mist that rolls over the land and blesses the earth. God knows that we all need His refreshing goodness, kindness, mercy, and grace to be part of our inner thinking, *our own heart nature.* But we must want it too!

God offers His goodness and love to all people freely, but it is up to everyone to freely accept these inner changes. We must drink in His nature, and want to have the same kind of heart. Whatever anyone does to avoid God, and His good will, results in self-destruction. Pleasures of sin are only for a season; **consequences are forever.** The consequences come to us by our own choice. Without true repentance through the sacrifice of Jesus, there is no way to escape the terrible results of our own wrong, bad, unwise, or evil choices!

The Book of Proverbs reveals many things about the love, goodness, and righteousness of God, the very nature of His heart. All of these characteristics were obvious in everything Jesus did on earth. Will our hearts change so that our behavior reflects the same love, goodness, and righteousness?

The expression *The fear of the LORD* begins verse 7 of Proverbs 1. There are fifteen Hebrew words in the Old Testament that are translated with the English word, *fear.* Proverbs uses five of these words, but the same word that is found here is used fourteen times, while the other four are used only a total of six times. One who is aware of the power of God without knowing His character of love **may be** afraid of Him. Verse 7 above does not mean to be afraid of God, but to *stand in reverent awe of Him.* When we come to know the awesomeness of God, we are then able to ***begin to know God.***

Solomon then tells us what this ***fear of the Lord*** means. It is the ***beginning of knowledge.*** True scientists do research *looking for the way something actually is.* They do not decide what the outcome of their research will be, but let the truth of the physical phenomena be revealed by their research. Awesome reverence for God makes it possible for scientists to accept whatever comes from their research. Those who want to modify their findings to "produce" another result set themselves up as god (notice the small letter "g"), and proceed to deceive the public.

There is a philosophy which teaches that "mankind" is the highest "life form" and, therefore, no other higher power is needed – *or wanted!* Such a philosophy is self-destructive, and if accepted will, in the long run, destroy the acceptor. Mankind has for generations struggled to gain the knowledge of *what exists in this world,* or *what has been created.* The result of honest research has brought many great things into use by all mankind: electric power and all its blessings, vaccines that prevent terrible diseases, automobiles, aircraft, huge nuclear powered ships, to name a few. We **stand in awe** of the universe in which we live; It is important that we respect the truth – it did not create itself. Mankind must continue to study and use what is learned for the good of all people. That is **the fear of the Lord which all of us must have!**

Solomon also describes the other side of this issue in the same verse when he said, **but fools despise wisdom and instruction.** Again, we, as human beings, have a choice to make – seek wisdom, seek understanding, seek knowledge – true wisdom and knowledge.

There are some people who refuse to open their minds and consider respectfully the concept of a Creator God. The result is a self-shutting-out of learning the truth about our world, our universe – especially the source of all life. We individually must choose to think reasonably about these things, rather than **despise wisdom and instruction.**

New Testament writers also call our attention to these concepts. James, the younger brother of Jesus, wrote about wisdom. He recognized that people will lack wisdom, but that we should ask God for it. Then he promised that God would give it generously, provided we seek it without doubting. But if we do not have that measure of constant trust, God will not grant wisdom to the **double-minded man.** A common expression we use today, "two-faced," may very well translate "double-minded." Such persons are considered by God to be "unstable." *All of us need to build our lives on the rock-solid foundation of God's eternal Truth!* (James 1:5 – 8).

God is never reluctant to pour out His blessings, but when we ask God for something, we must ask with a confident, trusting heart. It begins with our reverent fear, our respectful trust in God. What is the value of all this wisdom and knowledge? We can learn from Proverbs 2, but notice that the one who is seeking **the fear of the Lord,** and **the knowledge of God,** cannot do so haphazardly. What does God expect us to do to truly **fear the Lord** and **gain knowledge of God?**

All of these things God expects us to do are found in Proverbs 2:1 – 4: **accept** His words, **store up** His commands, **turn our ears** to wisdom, **apply our hearts** to understanding, and **look or search for it** as if it were silver or hidden treasure. Learning to respect the Lord God and gain knowledge of Him does not come easy. It requires a diligence of heart that perseveres in accepting His words, storing up His commands, listening to His teaching, digging deep until we gain understanding, and doing so as if we are searching for the most valuable thing on earth – **that is what it is!**

Consider this; God inspired Solomon to write as a father to his son. For what purpose? God so loves all people that He speaks on a one-to-one basis to every person who comes to Him. Conclusion: Proverbs 2 is written to each of us as individuals, urging us to **accept His words, store up His commands within us,** and take all these great truths into our hearts!

God desires to live in individual hearts by His Spirit (Ephesians 2:22). Jesus made a similar challenge in the third chapter of Revelation.

Revelation 3:20

Here I am! I stand at the door and knock.
If anyone hears my voice and opens the door,
I will come in and eat with that person, and they with me.

It is our personal responsibility to **hear His voice,** and **open the door.** Just as God expressed the desire to come into our hearts by His Spirit, Jesus is making it clear that we must listen to His words, and open the door, and the Spirit of God will come in and **"make Himself at home"** in our willing hearts.

When one reads the word of God, it should not be just to cover so many verses or chapters, but we should be **storing up God's commands.** Some of the thoughts of God are difficult to understand; we should diligently *cry aloud for understanding.* If we do not understand, we must keep **crying aloud** until we do understand.

As we study God's word, hear a sermon, or listen to a Bible teacher, do we consider gaining this knowledge as a very valuable thing, more valuable than silver or hidden treasure? When we honestly read God's word, Solomon promises – *then you will understand the fear of the LORD and find the knowledge of God* (Proverbs 2:5).

Remember the promise and the warning: *The fear of the LORD is the beginning of knowledge, but fools despise wisdom and instruction* (1:7).

Solomon does not give us a list of disjointed pearls of wisdom, but by the guidance of the Holy Spirit of God, he patiently ties these concepts together. The second chapter continues to relate more good results of diligently seeking God's wisdom and knowledge.

the LORD gives wisdom (v. 6)
He holds success ... for the upright (v. 7)
he is a shield (v. 7)
he guards the course of the just
and protects the way (v. 8)

This is what God does for those **who are upright, whose walk is blameless, who are just,** and are **His faithful ones.** What is the value of wisdom, knowledge, and understanding?

Proverbs 2:10 – 11

10 For wisdom will enter your heart,
and knowledge will be pleasant to your soul.

11 Discretion will protect you,
and understanding will guard you.

With wisdom and knowledge from the truth of the Creator God, we will be able to discern what is dangerous and avoid it. We will become aware of other undesirable situations *before they become trouble.*

Our faith grows stronger as we come to know more about the heart of God, the kind of heart Jesus wants to change us into.

Proverbs 3:3 – 4

3 Let love and faithfulness never leave you;
bind them around your neck,
write them on the tablet of your heart.

4 Then you will win favor and a good name
in the sight of God and man.

We went to Taiwan in 1959 with little understanding of the language or culture of the Chinese people. Teaching them that **God is Love** was not easy. They had difficulty understanding how God could hate sin and evil, and at the same time, love **all** people, *even evil people*. It is very difficult to *live that truth in our own culture!* We *are* not alone in struggling to grasp the complexity of God's love. But how are we to handle this divine **love and faithfulness** of God? Are we not to bind them around our necks and write them on the tablets of our hearts? Is that not the meaning of this Proverb?

Does God do this for us? No! We are responsible for continuing to search God's truth. This will insure that these truths are indelibly written onto our hearts. Did God create robots to do His will, or did He create us with a free will, responsible for our choices? God offers freely, but accepting or rejecting is our choice!

The *let, bind,* and *write* in verse 3 are all commands from God. We must not *allow (let) love and faithfulness* to leave us; we must *bind them around our necks;* and we must *write* these godly characteristics of *love and faithfulness* into our hearts. This can come only from diligent study of the heart of our loving God, our Father in Heaven, and the *Living Word, Jesus.*

What is the good of this kind of study? Where is the value in such diligent effort? Solomon answers both of these questions very clearly.

> *Then you will win favor and a good name*
> *in the sight of God and man.*

The Evil One will tempt us to focus on pleasing our fellow man and looking for his favor, rather than *winning favor and a good name in the sight of God,* first and foremost. When God's pleasure is the primary goal of our lives, the good name and favor of our fellow man will follow.

Proverbs 3:11 – 12

> *11 My son, do not despise the LORD's discipline,*
> *and do not resent his rebuke,*

> *12 because the LORD disciplines those he loves,*
> *as a father the son he delights in.*

All of us must learn not only to accept discipline from parents, or a teacher, or the rules of an employer, or the commands of a military leader, we must *learn to discipline ourselves.* This passage brings up several profound questions. Did God have to learn to discipline Himself? Did Jesus have to learn discipline from Joseph and Mary? Or, from the Jewish rabbis (teachers)? Or, did Jesus have to learn to discipline Himself? There is no answer for any of these questions, but Jesus has absolutely set before us a perfect example of self-discipline.

God does not tell lies. God does not hate people. God does not lose patience with those who do not follow His teachings, but pleads with us to repent. Jesus does not lie. Jesus never did hate anyone. The patience of Jesus in training His disciples was tried many times, but He still loved them. He prayed that God would forgive the Jewish leaders who condemned Him to death! **What powerful examples of self-discipline!**

We have already mentioned the need to accept discipline from others, those we live or work under; but how do we learn to discipline ourselves? And why is it so important? Living under the rules of others may seem unfair, but these rules are for our good. Accepting the discipline of others who love and care for us is a form of self-discipline. That kind of self-discipline enables us to accept the guidance of God.

This passage tells us to listen attentively to the Lord's teachings, accept His corrections of our behavior, and follow His guidance through dark and dangerous roads. Remember, **it is all because He loves us!** Again, accepting this discipline is our responsibility. If we do not accept the discipline our parents give us, we disappoint them. If we do not accept the discipline our teachers in school give us, we may not learn as we *need to learn*. If we do not accept the rules of the workplace or military leadership, we may lose our jobs or military rank, or worse.

Military discipline is extremely important. Your life and the lives of your friends depend on *each one doing his part.* Does the U.S. National Guard slogan, **No comrade left behind,** have a relationship to Christian teachings? *We are devastated when our children reject our guidance. We are distressed when a* *friend goes off the deep end and gets into serious trouble. These are people we know and love. The big question for believers is this: How really concerned are we for **all people** who are lost -- even those we do not know, or those who are our enemies?*

As followers of Jesus, we must listen to His teachings so carefully that we do not misunderstand, and that we do remain faithful ourselves. Unless our faith is strong, we will not *have the spiritual stamina to guide our children, encourage our friends, or reach out to the lost Jesus came to save.* When we do not accept the Lord's discipline, we are actually rejecting God and endangering our own families, *those we should love the most!*

The example we set before our families has a profound influence on the lives of our children which could continue for generations. It is God's discipline that saves and brings peace and confidence to our hearts. May we all **Listen and Learn from God!**

Proverbs 3:27 – 28

27 Do not withhold good from those to whom it is due, when it is in your power to act.

28 Do not say to your neighbor, "Come back tomorrow and I'll give it to you"— when you already have it with you.

What does the command, **Do not withhold good,** mean? It appears to be a very simple command, that is, until we ask about the full meaning of the word **good** as used here. How can you do good to someone else? Is giving food to a hungry person obeying this command? *No question!* Is picking up a package for an elderly lady doing good? *Positively!* Is it also doing good to comfort a crying child whose little dog just died? *Absolutely!* Are there not more than a thousand ways to do good? *Infinitely!*

A passage in the New Testament that has affected us, perhaps more than many others, is found in Matthew 25. In this parable of Jesus, the people were brought before God in judgment. The King, Jesus, came in glory, all the angels were with Him, and people of all the nations came together before His judgment throne (v. 31 – 33). His task was to separate the people into two groups: on the right were those who would be blessed. On the left were those who would not be blessed. What makes such an eternal difference in the two groups?

Those blessed by the Father will hear: *"Come . . . take your inheritance, the kingdom prepared for you since the creation of the world* (v. 34). If God planned this *inheritance kingdom* even before He placed Adam and Eve on the earth, then it must be very important to Him, and should be to us also. Jesus explained why He blessed them.

35 For I was hungry and you gave me something to eat,
I was thirsty and you gave me something to drink,
I was a stranger and you invited me in,

36 I needed clothes and you clothed me,
I was sick and you looked after me,
I was in prison and you came to visit me.

We do not remember when this passage first had such a profound effect. The righteous responded to Jesus with some startling questions. Their response reveals an attitude of heart that all of us urgently need – *eternity depends upon it!*

37 . . . Lord, when did we see you hungry and feed you,
or thirsty and give you something to drink?

38 When did we see you a stranger and invite you in,
or needing clothes and clothe you?

39 When did we see you sick or in prison and go to visit you?

Before we read the final words of Jesus to those on the right, let us take a brief look at those on the left. Jesus said the words that no one ever wants to hear from the Lord, *"Depart from Me . . . for I was hungry and you gave me nothing to eat . . . .* Those on the left had the same questions as those on the right, but there was a vast difference in what they had done in life!

This is the answer that Jesus gave those on the right. *". . . Truly I tell you, whatever you did for one of the least of these brothers and sisters of mine, you did for me."* (v. 40).

Have you ever thought about some of the other things that Jesus could have listed as reasons to please God? Consider the following as things that Jesus might have put on His list to "qualify" people for the **inheritance** prepared for those on the right: *I called for you to assemble for worship, and you did; I called for you to study God's word, and you attended a regular Bible class; I called for you to remember my body and my blood, and you did; I called for you to make disciples, and you did.* When we realized what Jesus **did not include in His list, we had a lot of re-thinking to do. Are the "not listed" things important? Yes!** Do we dare say that because Jesus did not list any of those activities, they will not be important on Judgment Day? This kind of thinking is dangerous and must be avoided completely.

What we need to understand is the difference in the attitudes of heart between the two groups. Those on the left did not do those things listed; those on the right did. Those on the right had the love of Jesus living in their hearts. Jesus, while on earth, could not stop seeing the sick, the lepers, the blind, the deaf, the demon-possessed, the lost – *the powerless, the ungodly, the sinners, God's enemies* – US! ALL OF US! All those on the right also *could not stop seeing* the sick, the lepers, the blind, the deaf, the demon-possessed, the lost – *and then doing what they could for them.*

Jesus preached some powerful lessons while on earth; He taught some parables that challenge our thinking over and over; He exposed the hypocrisy of the Jewish leaders; He wept over a grief-stricken family and He wept over the Jewish people as He entered Jerusalem for the last time; He forgave those who crucified Him; He prayed for all who come to Him in obedient faith to be one in Him as He and the Father are One; and He gave His blood to cleanse us all of sin. Powerful! Powerful! His teachings and prayers are unsurpassed, but if we miss His ministry to the poor, the sick, and all those in need, *we may just miss it all.*

Jesus said these people were **blessed by my Father,** and He listed the reasons they were blessed. What was their response? They asked, **Lord, when did we see you hungry and feed you . . . ?** When Jesus said, **I was hungry . . . I was thirsty . . . I was a stranger . . .** they thought He meant they had helped Jesus Himself in all those ways! So naturally, they asked **When did we . . . ?**

They did what they did from the heart for all the people in need that they met day-by-day. The love of Jesus was in their hearts and that love responded to the needs they saw – *that is the nature of the heart of Jesus.*

They had this love for people **bound around their necks,** and it was also **written on the tablets of their hearts!** They responded to the needs they saw with intentional action, not because they were commanded to do so, *but because their hearts could see that these people needed the love of Jesus and they shared it joyfully.*

"The King will reply, 'Truly I tell you, whatever you did for one of the least of these brothers and sisters of mine, you did for me'" (v. 40).

When we learn to do these things, as Jesus did during all of His ministry on earth, is this not Jesus training our hearts for loving action? In time, we also will learn to do them almost subconsciously, adding more and more of the good works God planned in advance for us to do. *Oh, how our eyes need to learn to see the needs of others!* Let us read Ephesians 2:10 again.

For we are God's handiwork, created in Christ Jesus to do good works, which God prepared in advance for us to do.

Many of the Proverbs of Solomon contain a true revelation of the heart and character of God. May the Proverbs we study now be a springboard into our learning more of the loving heart of God.

Proverbs 6:16 – 19

This Proverb contains seven things that God hates. In these four verses, hatred is directed at the misuse of something God created. Understanding how God hates evil is extremely important. It is our responsibility to use what God has given us in a way pleasing to God. Let us read the text and gain understandings.

16 There are six things the LORD hates, seven that are detestable to him:

17 haughty eyes, a lying tongue, hands that shed innocent blood,

18 a heart that devises wicked schemes, feet that are quick to rush into evil,

19 a false witness who pours out lies and a person who stirs up conflict in the community.

God directs His hatred toward wrong actions, the **wrong usage** of these six marvelous things God gave us: ***eyes, tongue, hands, heart, feet, and mind.*** Wrong thinking, the wrong use of the mind, will be involved in all seven detestable actions.

Haughty eyes looking down on others is the first detestable conduct on God's list. An arrogant person sees other people as beneath him. No wonder God hates such a wrong use of one's eyes!

It is not difficult to understand why our loving and merciful God hates it when one misuses his eyes, and *it is difficult for us to love an arrogant person.* Hating such behavior is not wrong, but loving (with agape love) the person with such an attitude is right, even though difficult. *This kind of love comes only by prayer and fasting!*

Misuse of the tongue is the second detestable thing in God's sight. Enoch often says, *"I do not know how your physiology works, but my tongue never decided by itself to tell a lie."* Any lie that is told begins in the heart. God expects us to control our tongues, and *He knows it is a very difficult task.* The Holy Spirit guided James to describe just how difficult controlling the tongue really is. He begins the third chapter by warning that those who teach will be judged more strictly, but that anyone who never is at fault in what he says is able to control all parts of his body (v. 1, 2).

James continues by telling how a bridle can control a horse, and how a rudder can turn about a huge ship, keeping it on course (v. 3, 4). He then states that the tongue is also a very small part of the whole body, but it is very boastful. James brings up another truth: a small spark can set a huge forest on fire (v. 5). How serious is the task of controlling the tongue? James tells us in verse 6.

The tongue also is a fire,
a world of evil among the parts of the body.
It corrupts the whole body, sets the
whole course of one's life on fire,
and is itself set on fire by hell.

154

From God's viewpoint, controlling the tongue is one of the most important tasks He gives to mankind. James says that mankind can tame all kinds of life forms on the earth, but a more basic, yet frightening, truth is given in verse 8.

**but no human being can tame the tongue.
It is a restless evil, full of deadly poison.**

He concludes by telling us many hypocritical acts the tongue can commit. As we come to understand what James has stated, we can also understand why God hates a lying tongue. *Whatever is in the heart comes out on the tongue – and controlling it is our difficult task.*

Enoch's story: "After returning home from World War II, I did not leave all my bad language back on my ship, but brought some of it home. One day I heard another "returning sailor" use some of that "salty language" and responded in kind. Then it hit me like a ton of bricks: *That kind of language does not please God, and I certainly do not want to use it in front of my parents, or especially, in front of a certain young Christian lady.*

'"As I walked away from that salty conversation, I made up my mind that I would not use that kind of language any more. I am so thankful that God has given me the strength to keep my resolution for over seventy-three years. There have been times when I was tempted to use that kind of language, and the temptation was strong. I tell this personal struggle to admit plainly that controlling my tongue was not easy. Many times I was tempted to lose control, but by the grace of God, I won the battle; *the victory belongs to Him!"*

People use the tongue in other ways which **God hates.** No one can improve on what the Holy Spirit guided James to write. We must remember God hates a *lying tongue.* Let God's truth reign!

Hands that shed innocent blood are third on the list of things God hates. Through the centuries, humans have used hand-held weapons to kill: swords, spears, daggers, guns, and . . . . Humans have also used their bare hands to kill. Hands are too often used to hurt without killing. Sometimes they pinch an arm, leaving an ugly bruise. A cruel man may lash out violently against *his wife or children, leaving them battered and bruised.* A few times the scene is reversed, and it is the husband who is the victim. *How can anyone who uses his or her hands to do such evil claim to be a Christian?*

How do we love people who behave like that? These "little" things are the beginning of violence that leads to the shedding of innocent blood.

Number four: Do you think God wants to live in **a heart that devises wicked schemes?** There was a mother who was unfaithful to her husband from a very early time in their marriage. He died from an accident at work, and soon after the mother began bringing her "boy friends" home; the four young children saw too much. When shopping she taught her children how to conceal small items, so that at check-out, she paid for a little, and carried out much. Hers was **a heart that devises wicked schemes.**

Thieves, cheaters, murderers, all use their hearts to devise ways to steal, cheat, and murder. God hates this kind of thinking, this perverted use of the mind. Wicked schemes lead a person to **rush into evil,** number five on God's list of hated behaviors.

Number six is the **false witness who pours out lies**. Every culture in every nation has people who will not admit guilt but always find someone else to blame. Some seem to love to twist the truth to incriminate an innocent person. **God hates that kind of behavior, that twisted, devious misuse of the mind.**

"Fake news" does not happen exclusively in the media; every-day conversation can contain opinions, disguised as facts, damaging the reputation of other people. There are three gates through which our words should pass: *Is it true? Is it kind? Is it necessary?* **God is pleased with those who control how they say what they say.**

There are some people who seem to be unable to tell the truth; their lies just flow out of their mouths. We must keep this firmly fixed in our minds: *God hates the false witnesses who pour out lies!*

God hates those who sow discord in a community; this is the climax of those seven things *God hates.* Why do people want to sow discord? A community is any group of people who come together for certain purposes, social, religious, political, business, etc. The reasons people sow discord are many. Some do it to tear others down. Some do it out of jealousy. Some do it to gain political power. God hates such despicable behavior; **all seven** of these terrible actions are an abomination to God.

Who controls what goes into the heart – the person himself, or God? God wants to live in the **willing heart** which invites Him in, the heart that is surrendered to Jesus to be transformed into His image. How can God live in a heart which is controlled by *any of these abominations?* Can we hate these evils as God hates them and still love and pray for that person captured by such evil thoughts and actions?

It is easy to hate the action, but difficult to love the actor. However, God wants to save all people, even those caught in the web of these seven hateful things. We must learn the heart of God, learn to hate evil. We also must learn to love people and want them to change their ways and come to know the love and forgiveness of God.

God always loves them but *He does not force anyone to change his behavior.* Throughout His Holy Word, God warns of the very serious consequences of sin. But *changing is up to us by fully trusting God and His Truth.*

Temptations may vary from person to person, but each one's responsibility is to use his strength to resist and overcome the alluring forces of evil. We must **look for and take** the way to escape which God provides.

1 Corinthians 10:13

No temptation has overtaken you except
what is common to mankind. And God is faithful;
he will not let you be tempted beyond what you can bear.
But when you are tempted, he will also provide a way out
so that you can endure it.

Proverbs 6 and 1 Corinthians 10 clearly reveal how much God is aware of our lives, and how He wants all of us to make the right choices.

Proverbs 8:20

I walk in the way of righteousness,
along the paths of justice,

This repeats two concepts already mentioned, but this verse is important because it states *I walk . . . .* God does not push or pull us with force except by the force of His truth. When believers stumble, God does not pick them up and put them back on the right path. He does keep His light shining on His pathway of righteousness and justice. God expects us to get up and go back to His lighted pathway, and He assures us that the blood of Jesus *keeps on cleansing us of our sins!* (1 John 1:7).

Is the Evil One able to take us out of God's love and protection? Absolutely not! However, if we decide to leave the safety of God's Holy Temple and return to our old life of sin and evil, *God will not stop us.* Returning to God's grace will be much more difficult, if not impossible. The Hebrew writer explains the dangers of turning back.

He begins by urging all of us to move beyond the basic teachings, not to stop obeying these elementary things, but if God permits *we will do* those basic teachings (Hebrews

6:1 – 3). But for those who have **once been enlightened, tasted the heavenly gift, shared in the Holy Spirit,** and **have tasted the goodness of the word of God and the powers of the coming age,** what should be a very disturbing statement is made – **It is impossible for those . . . who have fallen away, to be brought back to repentance.** This is not about most believers for few have met all those criteria. For one who has tasted the goodness of God's word – that could be most of us – he praises God. But God also knows all about our struggles every day in the war against evil, and *He knows that sometimes we will stumble.* His promise is clear – **the blood of Jesus keeps on cleansing us from sin** (1 John 1:7).

When believers deliberately make the decision to go back into the world, it is, **To their loss, they are crucifying the Son of God all over again and subjecting him to public disgrace** (v. 6b). Perhaps this will help us appreciate more and more each day *just how precious is the blood of Jesus to keep us clean.*

All of us are tempted to sin, and sometimes we stumble; God knows our hearts and recognizes when we are not deliberately denying Him. However, if we do deliberately leave, the text says, **It is impossible for those who have once been enlightened . . . to be brought back to repentance.** The important point is that the God of mercy understands the struggles we face, the temptations we must overcome.

However, the choice of action is our individual responsibility. We must not "play games" with God and take life lightly, thinking *I will repent and make it right before I die.* In other words, enjoy the pleasures of sin while young and repent in old age. This is denying the love and blessings of God, a choice to *live in and of the world as long as possible.* Remember the example of Moses. **He chose to be mistreated along with the people of God rather than to enjoy the fleeting pleasures of sin** (Hebrews 11:25). **Sinful pleasures do have their consequences!**

Proverbs 10:30

The righteous will never be uprooted,
but the wicked will not remain in the land.

This statement is powerful; anyone who has unreservedly accepted the truth of God cannot be taken away from His righteous path. It has always been left up to each one of us to *choose you this day whom you will serve* (Joshua 24:15).

Deuteronomy 30:19 – 20

19 This day I call the heavens and the
earth as witnesses against you
that I have set before you life and
death, blessings and curses.
Now choose life, so that you and your children may live

20 and that you may love the LORD
your God, listen to his voice,
and hold fast to him. For the LORD is your
life, and he will give you many
years in the land he swore to give to your
fathers, Abraham, Isaac and Jacob.

Our God has not changed His mind; He still encourages each one of us to choose life. Jesus opened His ministry by crying out to the people: *Repent!* He also warned that if we did not, we would all perish (Luke 13:1 – 5). Does that mean God is angry with us and wants to put us in hell? No, it means that we must, from our own free will, *make the choice to repent.*

Our faith has come because the truth of God has convinced us that what Jesus did for us is true; we willingly accept it. The command in Hebrews 10:25, *do not give up meeting together,* requires a choice on our part. We make behavior decisions every day, whether we realize it or not. God is begging us to trust Him and make choices He knows are right and good for us.

Godly behavior is encouraged throughout the Proverbs. Studying them does three things: one, they increase our understanding of the nature and heart of God; two, they strengthen our personal faith; and three, they describe the kind of behavior that pleases God.

Proverbs 31:8 – 9

8 Speak up for those who cannot speak for themselves, for the rights of all who are destitute.

9 Speak up and judge fairly; defend the rights of the poor and needy.

This passage describes many current political problems, but political problems are not our focus. There is a dichotomy between God's view and the world's view of life and how to live it. That is why there is such a difference in behavior between true believers and non-believers.

Believers in God care about those *who cannot speak for themselves,* and care *for the rights of all who are destitute.* They will *speak up and judge fairly,* and *defend the rights of the poor and needy.* But on the other hand, those who do not accept this God-given responsibility will ignore the needs of the poor and hurting.

God expects His people to defend the defenseless and to stand up for those who are being abused and treated unjustly. In those situations, we who follow Jesus must speak up. **Remaining silent is not an option.** Speaking up may bring on serious persecution and surely very strong opposition. As a people who have put their trust in God, we must not only speak up; **we must take action as we are able.** Living by this truth begins in our home, then to our friends, neighbors, and all God wants us to serve.

What Jesus said to the righteous ones in Matthew 25 hits home. Speaking up for those who cannot speak for themselves must become our inner nature, making us glad for the privilege. Also, we must learn to *judge fairly,* and *defend the rights of the poor and needy.* This is God's heart; this is the kind of *good works* that God expects His people to do **and keep on doing, as we see the needs of the poor, sick, and lonely.**

Proverbs 31:20

She opens her arms to the poor
and extends her hands to the needy.

Proverbs 31 is widely known because it describes a woman who is counted worthy by God. She is known for doing many things, some of which would be frowned upon, in certain cultures, as not suitable for "women" to do. But God seems to be quite pleased with her abilities and her heart.

Doing the good that God wants *His children of light* to do is much more than saying the words, *Go, may you be warmed and filled.* God wants us to put our whole being into accomplishing His goal. Understanding what this good wife did for the poor and needy helps us know God's heart. This is what He wants us to do with the same kind of caring, loving heart.

Proverbs 21:3, 13

3 To do what is right and just
is more acceptable to the LORD than sacrifice.

Urging us to do what *is right and just* occurs often in Proverbs, and is repeated here. Being *right and just* is who God is!

13 Whoever shuts their ears to the cry of the poor
will also cry out and not be answered.

This Proverb not only urges us to listen to the cry of the poor; it also gives us a warning. If our hearts are closed **to the cry of the poor,** God will close His ears to our cry. God wants us to have Godly ears, tuned to the needs of the poor. This includes conditions other than material poverty. Some wealthy people are spiritual paupers; their ears do not hear the cry of the poor or the hungry, and their eyes do not see the needs of the sick or the handicapped.

Many people are poor but what they lack is not obvious. Their need may be job training; they may need a care-giver for a sick family member; or they just may need temporary financial help. Our challenge is to develop *"Godly hearing ears and seeing eyes"* that can recognize those needs and respond with loving care.

Proverbs 21:21

Whoever pursues righteousness and love
finds life, prosperity and honor.

A family member of ours who passed away many decades ago, was considered to be a wealthy man. We knew him best when he was learning how to give to the good causes of Christ. He said this, referring to a wealthy friend of his, *"He just keeps on adding to his bank account and will die before he learns the joy of giving."* Was he realizing the truth of Proverbs 21:21? Without question!

Proverbs 22:9

The generous will themselves be blessed,
for they share their food with the poor.

Proverbs 22:22 – 23

*22 Do not exploit the poor because they are poor
and do not crush the needy in court,*

*23 for the LORD will take up their case
and will exact life for life.*

Paul developed this concept in more depth in Romans 12:17 – 21, but he includes most of Proverbs 25:21 – 22 in his message. He said do not return evil for evil, and be careful to do what is right before the eyes of everyone; and be at peace as much as it is in your power to do so. He reminds us that vengeance is God's work, not ours (v. 17 – 19). So, what is our task?

Proverbs 25:21 – 22

*21 If your enemy is hungry, give him food to eat;
if he is thirsty, give him water to drink.*

*22 In doing this, you will heap burning coals on his head,
and the LORD will reward you.*

The power of returning good for evil is in our hands. Do we realize or believe that *our acts of kindness in the face of evil will have that much positive effect on evil-doers?* It seems strange to think about how truly powerful God's word is *when we use it in faith!* Listen to his last words: **Do not be overcome by evil, but overcome evil with good.** Book Two of this **Trilogy of Clouds** will deal with the struggle all believers must engage in. Paul tells us that the **power to overcome evil is by doing good.**

In ancient times large stones were set at the boundary corners and moving them to infringe on an orphan's land was

164

the same as stealing. This stirred God's heart to defend the fatherless (Proverbs 23:10 – 11). Who is their **Defender?** Think about it.

When we learn to give to the poor, God promises that we will continue to be able to help the poor, but curses to those who **close their eyes to the cries of the poor** (28:27). Another similar situation is that righteous people want poor people to be treated justly, but **wicked people** are not concerned about justice or the poor (29:7).

As in all the other passages that tell us how Isaiah proclaimed the heart of the Messiah, the Proverbs tell us about the heart of God which He expects us to grow into. In all cases, we must make a decision to do or not do something good. Unless the heart motivates God-like action, it is not yet ready to serve God. God wants us to love, to care, to have compassion, to be fair, to do what we can; all of these are action words which *we must develop a skill in doing.*

The more we understand the concepts of the ministry of the Messiah, the more we realize that the texts go beyond fulfilled prophecy. These ministry texts also focus on **the heart and character of God, the Word that became flesh – *a man* whom all could see, touch, listen to, and know to be the Son of God, the Messiah.**

These words of the prophets become more and more personal to us; they tell us **who God is**, what He wants all of us to become! These texts are very individual, very personal, and very compelling. They challenge us to instill them into our hearts so that we can respond with the heart of Jesus to the opportunities we can see.

CHAPTER TWELVE

Prophecies of the Heart and Character of Jesus

Bailiff: *Present your findings from*

Isaiah

A significant part of the ministry of Jesus was His personal, loving care for the sick and the poor. However, Jesus came **to seek and save the lost** (Luke 19:10), His main ministry. On the other hand, we see that in His daily living He did not neglect the sick and needy. Isaiah 11:1 – 4 identifies both aspects of His ministry. The struggle against evil is not with swords or guns, but with the Sword of the Spirit, the Word of God. *Please, God, help us be true ministers of Jesus in every way we can – and when we are not able, may we strongly support those who are able – In Jesus' name. Amen.*

Isaiah begins by revealing that a descendant of Jesse would be filled with the Spirit of the Lord. He would have the Spirit of wisdom, understanding, counsel, and knowledge, all in strength. Furthermore, the fear (awesome respect) of the Lord would be his delight; His judgment would come from more than external observations (11:1 – 3). His great loving attitude toward the needy and poor is revealed in verse 4, and the powerful means of slaying the wicked is made plain.

Isaiah 11:4

but with righteousness he will judge the needy,
with justice he will give decisions
for the poor of the earth.
He will strike the earth with the rod of his mouth;
with the breath of his lips he will slay the wicked.

The apostle Paul verifies the same truth as he also describes the most important weapon in the arsenal of the Christian soldier – *that which Jesus used!*

2 Thessalonians 2:7 – 8

7 For the secret power of lawlessness is already at work;
but the one who now holds it back will continue to do so
till he is taken out of the way.

8 And then the lawless one will be revealed,
whom the Lord Jesus will overthrow
with the breath of his mouth
and destroy by the splendor of his coming.

The honor and respect Jesus had for His Father is seen in many of the things He did on earth, but the clearest one is that *He willingly allowed the Jewish leaders and Roman soldiers to crucify Him.* In Gethsemane, Jesus prayed the same prayer three times, while His disciples were struggling to stay awake. Jesus knew death awaited.

The Jewish leaders and many of the ordinary people were looking for a Messiah who would, with the Messiah's military forces, drive the Roman rulers back to Rome. Now God did not have in His plan a physical war, but one of the heart and mind. This battle is truly a life and death struggle *for all believers.* If one does not listen to His loving but firm words with careful attention, that one *may lose the war!*

Paul's words reveal a different kind of warfare from what the Jews expected the Messiah to fight. Jesus came to teach us how to fight in that different way. In the struggle between good and evil, the Truth of God in our hearts **gives us the power to prevail** over the forces of evil. Jesus overcame evil by the **breath of his mouth.** When we allow the truth of God's Holy Word to live in our hearts, we are then prepared to fight in the same way, with His Word of Truth, the Spirit's Sword. This is the character and heart of Jesus. When we put sin to death and turn our lives over to Jesus, He will remake us into His image, *with His character and heart.*

Matthew 26:39

Going a little farther, he fell with his
face to the ground and prayed,
"My Father, if it is possible, may
this cup be taken from me.
Yet not as I will, but as you will."

How did Jesus **delight in the fear of the LORD** (Isaiah 11:3)? The word *fear* has many meanings, but in this context, the meaning is *to stand in reverent awe of someone greater, especially to stand in **awe of God***. It does not mean *afraid,* as when a lion is about to attack you. There is no joy in that kind of fear.

Jesus knew God was with Him, and that He would raise Him up on the third day. That kind of confident trust can be ours, and it will bring us joy. Our faith must grow into this kind of eternal joy which the world can never take away. The following two passages concern this joy; they are part of the last words of Jesus to His disciples before He was betrayed. He had already told them He would die very soon, words that troubled them greatly. But these were words of comfort and hope, which reveal the inner being and genuine character of Jesus, which they understood after Jesus arose.

John 15:9 – 11

9 "As the Father has loved me, so have I loved you.
Now remain in my love.
10 If you keep my commands,
you will remain in my love, just as
I have kept my Father's
commands and remain in his love.

11 I have told you this so that
my joy may be in you and that your joy may be complete.

Jesus told them plainly, not in figures of speech, that He would be crucified, filling their hearts with grief, sorrow, and disappointment. He promised them their grief would be turned into joy. We need to wear the sandals of the disciples and walk away from that blood-stained cross as Joseph carried the dead body of Jesus toward his tomb. Their world was crashing down on them. *How could there be any joy in all of this grief?*

For the rest of that Friday, all of the Sabbath day, and into the afternoon of the first day of the week, the grief and confusion continued. The details of the events during this time are presented in chapters seventeen and eighteen.

John 16:22

So with you: Now is your time of
grief, but I will see you again
and you will rejoice, and no one will take away your joy.

The resurrection of Jesus brought joy to the hearts of His disciples, so much so that they were willing to give their lives for him. Only John lived to be an old man. Tradition has it, with some concrete evidence, that all the rest suffered death for taking the gospel to the world. The character of Jesus was absorbed by His disciples. *How are we doing today? Are we filled with the joy that Jesus wants all of His disciples to have?*

What did Isaiah say above about the Spirit within the Messiah? He prophesied that righteousness and justice would be the guiding principles in His care for the poor and needy. You will find these attributes of Jesus throughout the New Testament. **The Spirit of the Lord will be upon Him.** The forces of evil will be slain by the **breath of His lips.** The words that Jesus spoke to His disciples, and to all of us, **are Spirit and are life** (John 6:63).

We remember twelve-year-old Jesus in Jerusalem, carrying on a conversation with the teachers in the temple. Luke records, **Everyone who heard him was amazed at his understanding and his answers** (2:47). When Jesus displayed such understanding to the "scholars of Israel," why did they not ask, *How did this child come to have such understanding?* Did they, as most adults, discount the words of Jesus because, after all, from their mind-set, *Jesus was only a child?*

Those who listened to Jesus, *as an adult,* also were wondering how the son of the carpenter, Joseph, had such great knowledge, wisdom, and understanding.

Luke 4:22

*All spoke well of him and were amazed
at the gracious words that came from his lips.
"Isn't this Joseph's son?" they asked.*

Matthew 13:55

*"Isn't this the carpenter's son? Isn't
his mother's name Mary,
and aren't his brothers James,
Joseph, Simon and Judas?"*

Jesus, *in their eyes*, was a carpenter's son; perhaps they thought He could not have had the privilege of studying in a synagogue. A similar question was recorded by John in his gospel (6:42a).

He is only a child – He is only the son of a carpenter – He is only someone whose parents we know – all prejudiced the hearers into belittling the Truth that was staring them in the face.

Human weakness, the urge to categorize people different from ourselves as inferior, is strong, and caused many troubles for the Jews as it does for us today. The serious problem the Jews faced was: the failure to ask the right questions **from the evidence they had seen and heard.** The proof could have been seen by His wisdom, by the sick He had healed, by the blind He enabled to see, by His feeding 5000 with a small boy's lunch, and by His raising the dead. This undeniable evidence boldly declares – **Jesus absolutely has the power of God within Him!** But in spite of the strength of this vast evidence, they still would not change their attitude toward Jesus.

Many of these people *were among the 5000 who had been filled the previous evening by the five barley loaves and two fish!* Not only were they eyewitnesses, they were "stomach-filled" participants in the event itself! Yet they still asked, "**How can he now say, 'I came down from heaven'?**" (John 6:42b). How many other miracles had they seen and yet did not believe that *it was God who was with Jesus?* God was truly with Jesus in His youth, in His ministry, in His suffering and death, and in His resurrection *to live forever!* Those leaders had eyes to see but could not see – or *chose not to see!*

How powerful is the love of Jesus? Answering this question cannot come from a textbook, or a class discussion of the correct definition; it must come by observing what God *has done*, what Jesus *has done*. Love is best expressed in action, one person for the good of another person – and Jesus set the greatest example.

Romans 5:6 – 11

6 You see, at just the right time, when
we were <u>still powerless,</u>
Christ died for the <u>ungodly.</u>

7 Very rarely will anyone die
for a righteous person, though for
a good person someone
might possibly dare to die.

8 But God demonstrates his own love for us in this:
While we were <u>still sinners,</u> Christ died for us.

9 Since we have now been justified
by his blood, how much more
shall we be saved from God's wrath through him!

10 For if, while we were <u>God's</u>
<u>enemies,</u> we were reconciled
to him through the death of his Son, how much more,
having been reconciled, shall we
be saved through his life!

11 Not only is this so, but we also boast in God
through our Lord Jesus Christ, through whom
we have now received reconciliation.

The heart of Jesus is made very plain in these few verses. First, notice the kind of people who lived in the world at that time. They were *still powerless, ungodly, still sinners, God's enemies!* **Are we any different today?** How can anyone, *even God,* love such people? Until we grasp the tremendous love that Jesus has for all people – those who were *still powerless, ungodly, still sinners, and enemies of God* – we cannot know the heart of Jesus. Our true submission to Jesus, allowing Him to transform us into His image, is vital. **We cannot live without the heart of Jesus.**

CHAPTER THIRTEEN

Prophecies of the Rejection and Betrayal of Jesus

Bailiff: *Please present your findings from*
Isaiah, Psalms, Zechariah

The fifty-third chapter of Isaiah contains many ideas that connect to Jesus, the Messiah. In verse 3 we learn some of the ways His own people, the Jews, would reject Him, without cause.

Isaiah 53:3

He was despised and rejected by
mankind, a man of suffering,
and familiar with pain. Like one from
whom people hide their faces
he was despised, and we held him in low esteem.

The entire fifty-third chapter of Isaiah is considered to be all about the Messiah, and rightly so. The kind of treatment Jesus received at the hands of the mob of Jewish people and Roman soldiers is shameful, but *we need to recognize that is the way people who reject God behave today.* Shameful behavior is expressed in different ways in our present culture. When anyone stands up and opposes wrong-doing, he is attacked without reason. But the attacks against us today are but a pale imitation of the horrific suffering that Jesus endured for our sake.

Jesus understood what He was up against, but He did what God wanted Him to do: **offer Himself on our behalf, yes, and we must be thankful. He also offered Himself for the very people who did terrible things to Him.** We realize how unworthy we are; yet Jesus died for every person on earth, and even for the "drive-by" shooter. We must believe and not forget that God loves unworthy people. *We must remember that God, who loves all sinners, still* **hates evil!**

There are a number of passages we could present as evidence of the accuracy of Isaiah's prophecy, but one is very specific.

John 1:11

He came to that which was his own,
but his own did not receive him.

Great crowds followed Jesus in the early days of His ministry, but when the trial of Jesus came, the shouting of the leaders to *"Crucify Him!"* generated fear and a mob mentality in the hearts of the common people. His few remaining followers also felt a great disappointment and confusion; they were sure that the Messiah was dead. About 120 stayed together after the crucifixion.

Their hopes died when Jesus died. They had followed Him for over three years, and were sure He had to be the Messiah, but now they were bewildered and depressed. Does this not help us see the meaning in Isaiah 53:3 more clearly? Had we been alive and present at that time, we might have been with the disciples, bewildered and depressed. But we just might have been in the crowd rejecting Him, or even worse, crying out, **Crucify Him!**

The rejection of Jesus was a culmination of events that began early in His ministry. He chose His twelve special friends, and spent every day with them, talking, teaching, and demonstrating God's perfect love to them. Some of the teachings of Jesus were very difficult, even for the twelve, and at one point in His ministry Jesus asked them if they wanted to leave Him as some others had done. Peter's reply was unhesitating, saying basically, *There is no other place to go because **you have the words of eternal life*** (John 6:68). Then Jesus said a surprising thing to the twelve, **"Yet one of you is a devil"** (v. 70). And Judas was there with them.

Psalm 41:9

Even my close friend, someone I trusted,
one who shared my bread, has turned against me.

The gospels of Mark (14:10 – 11) and Luke (22:1 – 6) describe the treachery of Judas. Jesus had just finished washing the feet of His disciples, including Judas, and He spoke words which shocked them. With a troubled heart, Jesus said to His disciples: **"Very truly I tell you, one of you is going to betray me"** (John 13:21b).

The apostles were appalled, and wanted to know who the betrayer was. When John asked Jesus, the Lord privately identified Judas as the one. They all knew that Judas took money from their common money bag, but they did not expect him to betray Jesus. When Judas left the room, the others assumed it was to take care of some legitimate matter.

Jesus has many things to teach us. Our wondering why Jesus chose Judas is not important; there are some things we do not need to know. What we have learned about the loving, compassionate heart of Jesus compels us to believe that He

177

forgave Judas in His prayer on the cross. In today's world, we should deal with a thief and betrayer *from God's viewpoint.* Judgment belongs to God, and God always does what is fair and just, whether we understand it or not.

We do not know how far in advance Judas had the idea to betray his friend, but it was not a sudden decision. There are very specific prophecies about the negotiations between Judas and the Jewish leaders. Zechariah gives some interesting details of what would happen before the actual treachery. One, the price of the betrayal will be negotiated. Two, the amount is specific, thirty pieces of silver.

Zechariah 11:12

I told them, "If you think it best, give
me my pay; but if not, keep it."
So they paid me thirty pieces of silver.

Matthew describes the fulfillment of this part of Zachariah's prophecy. Chapter 26 is very clear about Judas and his negotiations with the chief priests. *"What are you willing to give me if I deliver him over to you?"* And the priests handed over *thirty pieces of silver* to Judas (v. 15). *From then on Judas watched for an opportunity to hand him over* (v. 16).

When Judas and Jesus met the next time, it was in the Garden of Gethsemane, known by the apostles as a place Jesus often went for prayer. Judas was not alone; *the chief priests, the teachers of the law, and the elders* of the Jewish people had sent a crowd of people *armed with swords and clubs* (Mark 14:43). When Judas saw Jesus, he called Him "Rabbi" and, as planned, kissed Him. Jesus was seized and arrested.

Not much is written about Judas after the arrest of Jesus. We can read enough to know that he was truly conscience-stricken and deeply sorry for what he had done.

Zechariah 11:13

And the Lord said to me, "Throw it to the potter"—
the handsome price at which they valued me!
So I took the thirty pieces of silver and threw them
to the potter at the house of the Lord.

When Judas saw that Jesus was condemned, he went to the chief priests and tried to return the thirty pieces of silver to them. *"I have sinned," he said, "for I have betrayed innocent blood." "What is that to us?" they replied. "That's your responsibility."* (Matthew 27:4).

His "partners in crime" among the Jewish leadership had gotten what they wanted, and Judas was of no further value – nor concern – to them. They rejected his offer to return the thirty pieces of silver (they called it "blood money"). They had no scruples about giving Judas money to betray Jesus, but when a penitent Judas tried to return it, they suddenly developed some amazing scruples! They decided to use it to buy a potter's field, for a burying place for foreigners, which was just as prophesied.

Judas threw the coins on the temple floor, then left alone to find a secluded place to kill himself.

Jesus sacrificed Himself – **once** – **for all!** This fulfilled God's plan for saving all mankind. By offering Himself freely, Jesus endured immense, shameful suffering, yet refused to use His power to call for the angels of heaven to rescue Him. For the Jewish leaders and the Roman soldiers, this was a crucifixion; but for Jesus, this was an offering to God. This is the power of God's love!

By freely giving Himself, Jesus showed His love for lost people. At one time or another, we have all been lost, caught up in a web of evil – of selfish **desire**. That is why Jesus came to this earth – *to seek and to save that which was lost!*

Offering animal sacrifices was an integral part of Jewish worship. However, the Hebrew writer reminds us that the blood of bulls and goats cannot take away sin; it can only *remind us* of our sins (Hebrews 10:1 – 4). And then he tells us **we have been made holy through the sacrifice of the body of Jesus Christ once for all** (10:10).

After the apostles saw Jesus ascend to the Father in Heaven, they returned to Jerusalem to meet together and pray. Joining them were the women, including Mary, the mother of Jesus, and His brothers; within a few days there were about 120 believers who joined them. (Acts 1:12 – 15). There they prayed. Remembering the instructions of Jesus, they waited in Jerusalem for the promised gift of the power of the Holy Spirit (Luke 24:49; Acts 1:8).

Peter spoke with them about Judas, who had acted as guide for those who arrested Jesus. Peter described the death of Judas and quoted prophecies from two of the Psalms that David wrote. **May his place be deserted; let there be no one to dwell in it** (Psalm 69:25). Another prophecy foretold that another would **take his place of leadership** (Psalm 109:8).

The number twelve appears many times in the Old Covenant, most of the time referring to the twelve tribes of Israel. When Jesus chose twelve disciples, He chose one who had a problem with stealing. John even called him a thief (John 12:4 – 6). When Judas took his own life, only eleven special disciples were left. For some reason, known only to God, it was important to maintain twelve disciples to serve as apostles.

Luke recorded the action they took which fulfilled the prophet's words. The man to be chosen must have **been with us the whole time the Lord Jesus was living among us, beginning from John's baptism to the time when Jesus was taken up** (Acts 1:21b – 22a). This man was to **become a witness with us of His resurrection** (Acts 1:22b).

Two men, Justus and Matthias, met those qualifications; they were placed before the Lord for His consideration. The disciples prayed fervently to God for wisdom and guidance, then they cast lots. In this way, Matthias was chosen and he took his place with the eleven. It is clear that Jesus wanted twelve apostles to carry out His very special work.

The sound of a **rushing, mighty wind** got the attention of many people who were in Jerusalem to celebrate the Day of Pentecost. They had come from many countries and spoke many different languages. The Holy Spirit had fallen on the apostles with power, and they, all Galileans, began to speak to the gathering crowd. The listeners were amazed as they realized that each person was hearing what was said *in each one's own native tongue!* Most were astonished at what they were experiencing, but a few said the speakers were drunk on new wine (Acts 2:1 – 13). Then Peter arose and spoke to the crowd in a loud voice.

Peter began by pointing out that nine o'clock in the morning is too early for anyone to be drunk, then began a most powerful, convincing message. He reminded them of the words of Joel (2:28 – 32) who prophesied events that took place at the very time Jesus died (Joel 2:31; Acts 2:20). Peter then specifically addressed the **Men of Israel,** and charged them with enlisting the help of wicked men to crucify Jesus, the One who had performed many miraculous signs and wonders in their presence, *and they knew these things had taken place.* Peter then told them that God had raised Him from the dead. Again, Peter quotes a prophet, this time from David, who said that the body of the Messiah would not see decay (Psalm 16:10; Acts 2:27). He assured this vast audience that David was not speaking of himself because the tomb of David was still available for all to see. Peter then made a strong statement, testifying to the resurrection of Jesus, again quoted the words of David, **The Lord said to my Lord . . .** indicating the Messiah (Psalm 110:1; Acts 2:34, 35). Peter then challenged them all.

Acts 2:36

"Therefore let all Israel be assured of this:
God has made this Jesus, whom you crucified,
both Lord and Messiah."

The response was immediate – they were *cut to the heart* and cried out – *Brothers, what shall we do?* Many of those listening to Peter had also been in Jerusalem when Jesus was crucified, and knew the message was a direct accusation. It is possible that some of them had been in the mob that cried out, *"Crucify Him! Crucify Him!* But three thousand of that startled crowd listened and responded to the answer Peter gave in Acts 2:38.

. . . Repent and be baptized, every one of you,
in the name of Jesus Christ for the
forgiveness of your sins.
And you will receive the gift of the Holy Spirit.

Peter continued with many more words, both warning them and pleading with them to *Save yourselves from this corrupt generation* (v. 40). Where did Peter and the apostles get all this knowledge about the prophets? We know that the power they had came from the Holy Spirit as Jesus promised, but their knowledge about the prophets could have come from three places: one, the three years of sitting at the feet of the Master Teacher, Jesus; two, from the guidance of the Holy Spirit; or three, both.

The preaching and teaching of Peter and the apostles brought many more to obedient belief. Three passages tell us: *the number of men grew to about five thousand* (4:4), more and *more men and women were added to their number* (5:14), and the increase was rapid as *a large number of the priests became obedient to the faith* (6:7).

It is no wonder that three thousand souls were immersed into Christ Jesus on that day of Pentecost! Peter made it very plain for that large crowd, and for many more in the weeks, months, and years that followed. That powerful, precious message of love, mercy, and forgiveness has come down to every generation for two thousand years – *even for us today!*

Jesus is both Lord and Messiah!

CHAPTER FOURTEEN

Prophecies of the Trial, Suffering, Humiliation of Jesus

Bailiff: *Please present your findings from*

Psalms, Isaiah, Zechariah

Jewish leaders could not find any justifiable charge against Jesus, so they persuaded some people to give false testimony. In Psalm 27 and Psalm 35 David spoke about false witnesses. His suffering and persecution by Saul closely parallel the sufferings of Jesus. David had been a faithful soldier for King Saul, but Saul's jealousy drove his unreasonable attempts to kill David. The similarities from these two Psalms are striking.

Psalm 27:12

Do not turn me over to the desire of my foes, for false witnesses rise up against me, spouting malicious accusations.

Psalm 35:11

*Ruthless witnesses come forward;
they question me on things I know nothing about.*

That is the nature of false witnesses; they raise questions that do not fit the purpose, leaving themselves open to contradictions They make false accusations but offer no proof. This is typical behavior for those who falsely accused Jesus. The chief priests and the whole council of Jewish leadership made a determined effort in their search for witnesses. However, the testimony of those who came forward would not stand up – *even among themselves*. There were two who told the truth; but it exposed their own lack of understanding of the words of Jesus.

Finally two came forward 61 and declared,
"This fellow said, 'I am able to destroy the temple of God and rebuild it in three days.'" (Matthew 26:60b, 61).

The words are correctly quoted, but Jesus had used a figure of speech, the meaning of which they either could not grasp or purposely ignored. He was not talking about the actual temple structure, but the temple of His own body. Jesus was actually predicting they would kill Him, but God would raise Him after three days.

62 Then the high priest stood up and said to Jesus,
"Are you not going to answer? What is this testimony that these men are bringing against you?"

63a But Jesus remained silent.

Isaiah 53 contains a number of accurate descriptions of Jesus as the Messiah. Notice how accurate the following verse is.

Isaiah 53:7

He was oppressed and afflicted,
yet he did not open his mouth;

he was led like a lamb to the slaughter,
and as a sheep before its shearers is silent,
so he did not open his mouth.

What good would it have done if Jesus had tried to explain what He really meant? He knew they were going to crucify Him no matter what He might say. The prophecy does not mean that Jesus would never say a word at all, but when the false charges were made, He would remain silent – and He did. He did not try to correct the high priest, or any of the false witnesses.

63 . . . The high priest said to him,
"I charge you under oath
by the living God: Tell us if you are
the Messiah, the Son of God."

64 "You have said so," Jesus replied.
"But I say to all of you:
From now on you will see the Son of
Man sitting at the right hand
of the Mighty One and coming on the clouds of heaven."

Jesus spoke the truth even though He knew they were not looking for the truth, but for an excuse, any excuse, to kill Him. The response of the high priest follows.

65 Then the high priest tore his
clothes and said, "He has
spoken blasphemy! Why do we
need any more witnesses?
Look, now you have heard the blasphemy.

66 What do you think?"
"He is worthy of death," they answered.

*67 Then they spit in his face and
struck him with their fists.
Others slapped him 68 and said,
"Prophesy to us, Messiah. Who hit you?"*

Isaiah prophesied many humiliating actions against the Messiah, just as Matthew has described.

Isaiah 50:6

*I offered my back to those who beat me,
my cheeks to those who pulled out my beard;
I did not hide my face from mocking and spitting.*

The following are some of the passages which describe the fulfillment of this prophecy: Mark 14:53 – 65 gives many details; John 18:22 records how an official of the High Priest struck Jesus in the face; Mark 15:16 – 20 describes in detail how the soldiers mocked Him, made a crown of thorns, and beat the thorns into His head with rods. The barbaric torture Jesus suffered before His crucifixion should make us cringe in horror. At the same time, we should be filled with deep gratitude for the fathomless love Jesus has for *everyone* on this earth.

We must never forget that all the suffering Jesus endured was for our sake, our salvation. This is the plan God made to forgive our sins through the shed blood of Jesus. *How great and how full of grace and mercy is our God!*

Psalm 22:16

*Dogs surround me,
a pack of villains encircles me;
they pierce my hands and my feet.*

188

David surely saw the "dogs" and "villains" in Saul's pursuit of him. But David's hands and feet were never pierced. Part of the verse fits David's situation, but the whole passage applies to the Messiah.

The Jewish leaders and Roman soldiers acted like **dogs** and a **pack of villains;** but the frenzied crowd, crying out **Crucify him,** may also have sounded like a pack of dogs. John describes the fulfillment of this prophecy in two passages.

John 19:37

and, as another scripture says,
"They will look on the one they have pierced."

John 20:27

Then he said to Thomas, "Put your
finger here; see my hands.
Reach out your hand and put it into my
side. Stop doubting and believe."

We do not know how many people heard Jesus tell Thomas what to do, but the eleven apostles present heard, understood, and spent their lives testifying to this truth. History tells us that all but John were martyred; he was exiled to the isle of Patmos in his later years.

Zechariah 12:10

"And I will pour out on the house of
David and the inhabitants
of Jerusalem a spirit of grace and
supplication. They will look on me,
the one they have pierced, and they will mourn for him

as one mourns for an only child,
and grieve bitterly for him
as one grieves for a firstborn son."

There are many prophecies concerning Jesus but we have looked at only a few. In Psalm 22 David, with Saul and his army searching everywhere for him, cries out to the Lord. These same words were used in mockery by the mob that crucified Jesus.

Psalm 22:6 – 8

6 But I am a worm and not a man,
scorned by everyone, despised by the people.

7 All who see me mock me;
they hurl insults, shaking their heads.

8 "He trusts in the LORD," they say,
"let the LORD rescue him.
Let him deliver him,
since he delights in him."

David was treated this way, especially as Saul searched to find and kill him. To a much greater degree, Jesus experienced the unrelenting dangers and threats of death, as the Jewish leaders conducted their vendetta against Him. There are two parts to this prophecy: one, what people did; two, what people said. What they did was **scorn, despise, hurl insults, and shake their heads.** All of this was intended to add emotional pain to His intense physical suffering on the cross.

The scoffers did not realize the irony of the situation; Jesus had the power to come down from the cross and utterly destroy every one of them. But God sent Jesus to save *even those who did and said these terrible things.*

They were making fun of something they did not understand: the tremendous trust in God that Jesus had. It was so great that He went willingly to the cross **because He knew God would raise Him from the grave.** But the mob did not understand this; they had no idea that Jesus was dying for each one of them as well. Those who cried out **"Crucify Him"** also claimed to **"trust in the Lord."** However, their traditions made them blind to the True God who came in the flesh to save us all from our traditions.

One of the benefits of reading the scripture texts is that we can see the deep faith of that *Great Cloud of Witnesses* from Hebrews 11 and all the other *Clouds.* We can see the strong faith of Jesus as He trusted God's power to raise Him from the grave. What a blessing for us!

o o o o o

Bailiff: *Please present your findings concerning*

Some Unusual Prophecies

This passage is not only unusual, it is also very contrary to the way people treat their enemies. Retribution, revenge, spite, hatred, and bitterness are just a few of the actions people can take against their enemies. Even though Jesus said *love your enemies,* we have a hard time thinking and acting that way (See Matthew 5:43 – 48). Returning good for evil is also a difficult teaching to follow every day (Romans 12:21). Behaving well only on Sunday morning is not what God is looking for. *What is God looking for?* Almost every Biblical passage tells us that God is looking for **"full time"** application of **His will.**

Psalm 109:4a

In return for my friendship they accuse me . . .

Many English translations of the Bible use the word *love*, rather than *friendship,* in this verse. The Hebrew dictionary lists both *love* and *friendship* as meanings. We have inserted both meanings in verse 4 as a means of expressing what the prophet wrote and what Jesus felt in His heart for all people, even His enemies: ***In return <u>for my loving friendship,</u> they accuse me . . . .*** We could rail at the Jews for their spiritual blindness, but it would be a case of criticizing them for the fault we forgive in ourselves. Many of us today also fail to allow God's love **to be the motivating factor** for all we do.

On the cross, suffering intensely, with a mob cruelly mocking Him, what did Jesus do? **He prayed!**

Father, forgive them,
for they do not know what they are doing
(Luke 23:34)

When the eleven remaining apostles heard this prayer from the cross, they must surely have recalled that Jesus, just a short time earlier, had told them about God's love.

John 15:12 – 14

12 My command is this: Love each
other as I have loved you.

13 Greater love has no one than this:
to lay down one's life for one's friends.

14 You are my friends if you do what I command.

For those who had tortured and crucified Him, Jesus prayed to God to **forgive them.** To those who had followed Him for over three years, He said He would lay down His life for them. We know that Jesus changes the hearts of willing believers, but are we ready to die for a friend, *or even an enemy?* God wants us to keep on growing our faith, allowing Jesus to continue to transform all willing believers into His image. Can we grasp the concept that God actually forgave all those who tortured and crucified Jesus? *Oh, how we need to come to know the heart of God, our merciful, loving, forgiving God!*

The soldiers who gambled for the clothes of Jesus were callous, hardened men. The context of the passage shows Jesus was not yet dead, so He saw them gambling for His clothes. But again, the Psalmist David writes about something that happened to Jesus, but not necessarily to David or anyone else.

Psalm 22:18

They divide my clothes among them and
cast lots for my garment.

Both John and Mark record the fulfillment of this prophecy. Read John's description of what the soldiers did with the clothes Jesus had been wearing.

John 19:23 – 24

23 When the soldiers crucified
Jesus, they took his clothes,
dividing them into four shares, one
for each of them, with the
undergarment remaining. This garment was seamless,
woven in one piece from top to bottom.

24 "Let's not tear it," they said to
one another. "Let's decide
by lot who will get it." . . . .
So this is what the soldiers did.

In another Psalm of David we learn about the deliverance of the righteous. Jesus is the only genuinely righteous person who ever lived. Without the grace and mercy of God, no one is counted as righteous, but these two verses concern the Messiah.

Psalm 34:19 – 20

*19 The righteous person may have many troubles,
but the LORD delivers him from them all;*

*20 he protects all his bones,
not one of them will be broken.*

John 19:33

But when they came to Jesus and found that he was already dead, they did not break his legs.

The crucifixion of Jesus took place on a Friday; the beginning of the Sabbath day was rapidly approaching. The Jews believed it was wrong to leave a body on a cross on the Sabbath day and asked the soldiers to expedite the deaths. The soldiers broke the legs of the two thieves, but when they came to Jesus, they found He was already dead. But to be sure, one soldier thrust his spear into the side of Jesus.

What the soldier did may have been impulsive, but two things resulted. One, the soldier was sure that Jesus was dead; two, when both blood and water came out, it meant that Jesus had been dead for a while. From this, two things become quite clear. First, it silences those who say that Jesus only "swooned" and did not die. Second, David's words applied to more than just his own problem. His prophecy told what **did** happen to the Messiah, Jesus.

Isaiah wrote an unusual prophecy concerning the righteousness of the Messiah.

Isaiah 53:9

He was assigned a grave with the wicked,
and with the rich in his death,
though he had done no violence,
nor was any deceit in his mouth.

There are four parts to this prophecy. First, *He was assigned a grave with the wicked.* Luke described the two criminals who were executed with Jesus, one on His left and the other on His right (Luke 23:32, 33).

Second, Matthew relates how Joseph, a rich man who had become a disciple, buried Jesus in his own tomb. He went to Pilate and asked for the body of Jesus; Pilate ordered that it be given to him. After wrapping the body in a clean linen cloth, Joseph placed it in his own tomb which he had recently had cut out of a huge rock. He then rolled a very large stone over to cover the entrance and left (Matthew 27:57 – 60).

The third part of the prophecy in Isaiah 53:9 raises a question. Was Jesus ever violent? Jesus might be considered "violent" when he "cleansed" the temple courts. Is there anything that Jesus did which could be considered violent? He made a whip of cords and used it to drive out both sheep and cattle. He also turned over the tables of the money changers. This was a physical act, startling, but not violent. He spoke to the sellers of doves, evidence that He did not use the whip on people. If He had, He would have been arrested. This event is recorded in each of the four gospels: John 2:13 – 17; Matthew 21:12 – 13; Mark 11:15 – 17; and Luke 19:45 – 46.

Some may consider Jesus violent when He called the scribes and Pharisees *hypocrites* (most of Matthew 23). Was Jesus speaking the truth? Is *speaking the truth* a violent action?

Sometimes doctors have to inflict pain in order to heal. Is that violent action? Certainly not! Did Jesus *enjoy* using these harsh words? In the same twenty-third chapter of Matthew, the words of Jesus reveal *His intense longing* for Jerusalem.

Matthew 23:37

Jerusalem, Jerusalem, you who kill the prophets
and stone those sent to you, how often I have longed
to gather your children together,
as a hen gathers her chicks under her wings,
and you were not willing.

Fourth, when Jesus spoke in parables, some did not understand what He meant. Was Jesus being deceitful? No, He simply did not tell people things they were not ready to hear. Jesus asked deep questions. This caused people to ponder and struggle to understand, but that is not deceit. Satan is the deceiver; Jesus is the very opposite.

We have compared both the prophets and their words to events in the life of Jesus. By carefully considering both the words and the context of each prophecy, the evidence is overwhelming: this **Great Cloud of Witnesses, who reveal God at work through the generations, make it quite clear –** *Jesus is the Messiah!*

CHAPTER FIFTEEN

The Victories of Jesus

Introduction

Before we look at the prophecy of an amazing victory, let us examine some victories of Jesus which are excellent examples for us to follow. These victories are not on our list of fulfilled prophecies, but they will help us understand a very different kind of victory, a victory that comes from sound reasoning. Look closely; you will see that Jesus was a very good teacher. They called Him *Rabbi.*

In war, you batter the enemy until he surrenders, but Jesus had a better way.

o o o o o

Bailiff: *Please present your findings for*

Jesus, Victorious Over the Temptations of Satan

Matthew 4 records Satan tempting Jesus in three different ways.. If we want to follow in the steps of Jesus, we must pay close attention to **how** Jesus met and overcame each challenge from Satan.

Matthew 4:1 – 4

1 Then Jesus was led by the Spirit into the wilderness to be tempted by the devil.

2 After fasting forty days and forty nights, he was hungry.

3 The tempter came to him and said, "If you are the Son of God, tell these stones to become bread."

4 Jesus answered, "It is written: 'Man shall not live on bread alone, but on every word that comes from the mouth of God.'"

How long after you have eaten do you begin to feel hungry again? The answer will vary from person to person, of course. For some, it is getting hungry before time for the next meal. For others, especially older people, hunger may not come at all. But after forty days and nights? Satan temped Jesus to use His Divine power to change stones into bread when He was extremely hungry. Physical hunger did not drive Jesus as it did Esau, who sold his birthright for a bowl of stew (Genesis 25). Hunger is a powerful, driving force.

How did Jesus answer this temptation? He refused to use the power of God for His own needs! He said that bread alone is not enough, but that we are to live by **_every word_** *that* **comes from the mouth of God**. When a healthy person is hungry, he eats, he does not "nibble" at his food. The question for us is, *Do we nibble at God's word, or do we devour it fully?* May prayerful thinking about the following questions help us *not be "nibblers"* of God's word!

Is once a week Bible study enough to develop the faith of Abraham? Can one sermon supply what we need for our spiritual wars Monday through Saturday? (We missed it! We should have included Sunday – Satan does not ever sleep.) What needs to change? We need to change our perception that the Christian life is centered on Sunday activities. The Truth of God is that He wants us to live for Jesus every hour, every day. Changing our minds **must come before** we can change our behavior.

Do we have the individual courage and determination to make those changes? God has spoken much; are we listening and doing, or just nibbling? Or, much better, are we *hungering and thirsting* for **every word that comes from the mouth of God?** Jesus blessed **those who hunger and thirst for righteousness** (Matthew 5:6).

Hunger is a normal physical need all of us have – food and drink to keep our bodies strong. In I John 2:15 – 17, we are told three ways Satan tempts people. We are tempted by: one, the desires of the flesh; two, the desires that come from what we see; and three, the desires for status, recognition, or power. The author of the Hebrew Letter stated that Jesus was tempted in every way in which we are.

Hebrews 4:14 – 15

14 Therefore, since we have a great high priest who has ascended into heaven, Jesus the Son
of God, let us hold firmly
to the faith we profess.

15 For we do not have a high priest
who is unable to empathize with our weaknesses,
but we have one who has been tempted in every way,
just as we are—yet he did not sin.

Jesus knows what we face *every day* because He was also tempted at a time when He was very vulnerable. How hungry can you get after forty days? The second temptation targets the very human desire for self-glory.

Matthew 4:5 – 7

5 Then the devil took him to the holy
city and had him stand
on the highest point of the temple.

6 "If you are the Son of God,"
he said, "throw yourself down. For it is written:
"'He will command his angels concerning you,
and they will lift you up in their hands,
so that you will not strike your foot against a stone.'"

7 Jesus answered him, "It is also written:
'Do not put the Lord your God to the test.'"

Satan wanted Jesus to think, *Everyone will see that God is with me; they will be astonished when they see the Angels of God catch me.* But Jesus did not think that way. He knew that His death would be on a cross, not from a foolish test of God's love for Him. Jesus was not deceived by Satan; His trust in God is clearly demonstrated.

Another aspect of this temptation is that Satan wanted Jesus to "test" God. Jesus knew Satan's motive and said, **Do not put the Lord your God to the test.**

Do some of our prayers actually put God to the test? Consider this one: *Dear God, I need a better job. if You help me get one, I will go to church every Sunday.* This is also known as "bargaining" with God. Perhaps our prayers should be more like this: *Dear God, thank You for all You have given to me, and please help me use these blessings to help others and glorify You. In Jesus' name.* Notice the trust: there is no **"if"** in this prayer. (Politicians call it *quid pro quo*.)

Matthew 4:8 – 11

8 Again, the devil took him to a very high mountain and showed him all the kingdoms of the world and their splendor.

9 "All this I will give you," he said, "if you will bow down and worship me."

10 Jesus said to him, "Away from me, Satan! For it is written: 'Worship the Lord your God, and serve him only.'"

11 Then the devil left him, and angels came and attended him.

All that the eyes can see – the kingdoms (the nations and tribes of people) that Jesus came to save – are offered to Him, but Jesus said, **No!** How strong was this temptation for Jesus? The real choice Satan put before Jesus was between his way, the "easy" way, or, the way of suffering, pain, humiliation, and death on a cross. But as usual, Satan had a hook in his offer: ***If you will bow down and worship me.*** Jesus knew that under no circumstance does one bow down to the enemy! Worship Satan? *Not an option! The* unyielding reply Jesus gave Satan was, ***Worship the Lord your God, and serve him only.***

Jesus also demonstrated a truth that we need to practice in our **daily living.** James wrote about it with these words.

James 4:7 – 8

7 Submit yourselves, then, to God. Resist the devil, and he will flee from you.

8 Come near to God and he will come near to you.

201

In all three encounters Jesus was victorious over Satan by doing exactly what James has encouraged all of us to do: *Resist the devil, and he will flee from you.*

Notice that no blood was shed. Jesus won each of these contests by using the Truth of God. The result of these three contests is:

Jesus – 3; Satan – 0

o o o o o

Bailiff: *Please present your findings for* Jesus, Victorious over Attempts to Trick Him

Jesus was tempted in many ways including an effort by the chief priests and the Jewish elders to get Him to say something they could use against Him. They tried many ways to ensnare Him in His words or deeds.

Matthew 21:23 – 27

23 Jesus entered the temple courts,
and, while he was teaching,
the chief priests and the elders of
the people came to him.
"By what authority are you doing
these things?" they asked.
"And who gave you this authority?"

24 Jesus replied, "I will also ask you one question.
If you answer me, I will tell you by what authority I am
doing these things.

25 John's baptism—where did it come from?
Was it from heaven, or of human origin?"

They discussed it among themselves
and said, "If we say,
'From heaven,' he will ask, 'Then
why didn't you believe him?'

26 But if we say, 'Of human origin'—
we are afraid of the people,
for they all hold that John was a prophet."

27 So they answered Jesus, "We
don't know." Then he said,
"Neither will I tell you by what authority
I am doing these things.

The question of the chief priests and elders seems reasonable. However, they were not really looking for a true answer; they were trying to ensnare Him in His own words. But Jesus, knowing what was in their hearts, asked them a question.

In John 10, we learn that the miraculous things Jesus did in the presence of many witnesses, prove **that Jesus received His authority from God**. To tell them plainly in words would, in effect, lessen the impact of what they had all seen. By refusing to acknowledge the Divine Power driving those events, they were actually closing their minds to Jesus as the Messiah.

The question was not as simple as they might have expected, so they got off to themselves to talk it over. They found themselves in a dilemma. They finally responded, **We don't know.** Jesus also declined to tell them the source of His authority.

The very question they asked Jesus to answer is proof in itself that **what Jesus had done had to come from some authority higher than man**. The lepers were cleansed, the blind could see, the deaf could hear, and the most astonishing of all – Lazarus was called to come out alive from the tomb *in which he had been for four days.* But the chief priests and elders still wanted to get rid of Jesus. Was it because He did not fit their pre-conceived ideas of what the Messiah should be and do?

After that, they did not ask any more questions. Not one blow was struck and no blood was shed. The words of Jesus, used gently and kindly, silenced His adversaries.

Jesus – 1; Chief Priests and Elders – 0

o o o o o

Bailiff: *Please present your findings for*

Jesus, Victorious Over the Spies

Luke 20:20 – 26

20 Keeping a close watch on him, they sent spies, who pretended to be sincere. They hoped to catch Jesus in something he said, so that they might hand him over to the power and authority of the governor.

21 So the spies questioned him: "Teacher, we know that you speak and teach what is right, and that you do not show partiality but teach the way of God in accordance with the truth.

22 Is it right for us to pay taxes to Caesar or not?"

23 He saw through their duplicity and said to them,

24 "Show me a denarius. Whose image and inscription are on it?" "Caesar's," they replied.

204

25 He said to them,
"Then give back to Caesar what is Caesar's,
and to God what is God's."

26 They were unable to trap him in what he had said
there in public. And astonished by his answer,
they became silent.

The spies asked Jesus a question about paying taxes to Caesar, but before they asked their question they spoke words that pretended to honor Jesus, and perhaps put Him at ease or off guard. Their purpose was to trick Him into saying something contrary to their law. They did not realize how absolutely true their flattering words were. Jesus explained it this way.

Matthew 13:13 – 15

13 This is why I speak to them in parables:
"Though seeing, they do not see;
though hearing, they do not hear or understand.

14 In them is fulfilled the prophecy of Isaiah:
"'You will be ever hearing but never understanding;
you will be ever seeing but never perceiving.

15 For this people's heart has become calloused;
they hardly hear with their ears,
and they have closed their eyes.
Otherwise they might see with their eyes,
hear with their ears,
understand with their hearts and turn,
and I would heal them.'"

Though they spoke with complete misunderstanding of the true Jesus, the spies asked their question anyway. This demonstrates how clearly the prophets spoke; these spies **saw**, but did not perceive, and **heard**, but did not understand (Jesus quoted from Isaiah 6:9 – 10). It appears that their question only concerned paying taxes to Caesar, but their real purpose was to give Jesus a dilemma, to put him "between a rock and a hard place." But Jesus replied with that simple but amazing truth: *" . . . give back to Caesar what is Caesar's, and to God what is God's."*

For this Victory of Jesus, no blows were struck, no violence took place, and no blood was shed.

Jesus – 1; the Spies – 0

o o o o o

Bailiff: *Please present your findings for*

Jesus Victorious over the Pharisees and the Teachers of the Law

One of the more difficult challenges Jesus faced was the problem of a woman caught in the act of adultery. The teachers of the law and the Pharisees brought her to Jesus and asked Him a question, intending to trap Him. He was sitting down in the temple courts, teaching the crowd who had come to hear Him. *This crowd of people were silent witnesses of everything that happened.*

John 8:1 – 11

1 but Jesus went to the Mount of Olives. 2 At dawn he appeared again in the temple courts, where all the people gathered around him, and he sat down to teach them.

3 The teachers of the law and the
Pharisees brought in a woman
caught in adultery. They made her
stand before the group
4 and said to Jesus, "Teacher,
this woman was caught in the act of adultery.

5 In the Law Moses commanded
us to stone such women.
Now what do you say?"

6 They were using this question
as a trap, in order to have
a basis for accusing him.
But Jesus bent down and started to write
on the ground with his finger.

7 When they kept on questioning him, he straightened
up and said to them, "Let any one of
you who is without sin be the
first to throw a stone at her."

8 Again he stooped down
and wrote on the ground.

9 At this, those who heard begin
to go away one at a time,
the older ones first, until only Jesus was left,
with the woman still standing there.

10 Jesus straightened up and asked her,
"Woman, where are they? Has no one condemned you?"

11 "No one, sir," she said. "Then
neither do I condemn you,"

Jesus declared. "Go now and leave your life of sin."

Here is another contest between the Jewish religious leaders and Jesus. This time the teachers of the law and the Pharisees felt they had Jesus in a real trap. Jesus simply bent over from His sitting position and began to write on the ground with His finger. No one knows what He wrote, but what He said shattered their goal.

Let any one of you who is without sin be the first to throw a stone at her.

We human beings just do not like to admit guilt for our wrong-doings. Jesus called for the one *without sin* to cast the first stone. This exposed their self-righteousness. After a while, the oldest among them walked away; gradually, the younger men followed. Jesus, by His simple suggestion, helped every accuser to see himself as a sinner.

Of those who brought this woman, not one was left to cast a stone. How very important it is for us to recognize our own faults, then we can more deeply appreciate the sacrifice of Jesus. How precious it is to be forgiven by the blood of Jesus!

How did Jesus treat this sinful woman? First, He asked her where her accusers were, although Jesus already knew. He had seen them all walk away. Jesus had a strong message for her. He asked if there was anyone to condemn her, and she replied, *"No one, Sir."* Jesus responded:

"Then neither do I condemn you . . . Go now and leave your life of sin."

Jesus is not calling for the destruction of sinners, but for sinners to repent. The image of God as an "all-seeing-eye," waiting to catch us in sin and smash us, is contrary to the God who is Love. *Repentance is up to us, individually, and God is pleading with us to hear His call!*

Jesus gave the woman an opportunity to get her life back together, a victory *if,* and there is that big two-letter word again, **if she listened to Jesus and quit her life of sin.** *How do* **we** *treat those whom* **we** *have "caught in sin"?*

Conflicts in today's world are constantly stirred up by physical wars, cruelties, lies, unsubstantiated accusations, and other devious schemes. Not so with Jesus – He just loved the truth.

Jesus was victorious over His adversaries again, without a stone thrown, without any violence, and without a single drop of blood being shed.

Jesus – 1; Teachers of the Law and Pharisees – 0

o o o o o

Bailiff: *Please present your findings for*

Jesus Victorious over an Expert in the Law

Two parables of Jesus are known all over the world: the parable of **The Prodigal Son**, better named **The Loving Father,** and the parable of **The Good Samaritan**. Let us read about the event that led to Jesus telling this second parable.

Luke 10:25 – 29

25 On one occasion an expert in the law stood up to test Jesus. "Teacher," he asked, "what must I do to inherit eternal life?"

26 "What is written in the Law?" he replied. "How do you read it?"

*27 He answered, "'Love the Lord
your God with all your heart
and with all your soul and with all your strength and with
all your mind'; and, 'Love your neighbor as yourself.'"*

*28 "You have answered correctly," Jesus replied.
"Do this and you will live."*

*29 But he wanted to justify himself,
so he asked Jesus, "And who is my neighbor?"*

Remember that the question was raised by an expert in the Jewish law. His purpose was to "test" Jesus. He wanted Jesus to give an answer that could be used to accuse Him before the chief priests and the Roman governor. Notice the question he asked Jesus is one we all must ask and seek an answer for ourselves: "**What must I do to inherit eternal life?**"

Undoubtedly, Jesus could have given him a very clear answer; instead, He asked the prominent lawyer to answer his own question. Jesus frequently used this excellent teaching device. He asked the lawyer, **"What is written in the Law? . . . How do you read it?"** This expert in the law answered quickly.

*"'Love the Lord your God with all your
heart and with all your soul
and with all your strength and with all your mind'; and,
'Love your neighbor as yourself.'"*

Jesus gave the lawyer a good grade when He said, **"You have answered correctly,"** then Jesus added this command,

"Do this and you will live."

Perhaps the lawyer had some idea that his own behavior might not be in harmony with what he knew the scripture taught, so he asked, **"And who is my neighbor?"** This lawyer wanted to justify his own actions.

At this point, Jesus did not ask him to answer his own question, but decided to tell him a parable. As the lawyer listened, he found strong words that described serious problems with his and his people's traditional ways. What Jesus said to him were clear words of truth, and the lawyer's later response indicated he knew what Jesus said was true. This parable challenged the lawyer deeply.

Luke 10:30 – 37

30 In reply Jesus said: "A man was
going down from Jerusalem
to Jericho, when he was attacked by
robbers. They stripped him
of his clothes, beat him and went
away, leaving him half dead.

31 A priest happened to be going
down the same road, and when
he saw the man, he passed by on
the other side. 32 So too,
a Levite, when he came to the place and saw him,
passed by on the other side.

33 But a Samaritan, as he traveled,
came where the man was; and when he saw him,
he took pity on him.

34 He went to him and bandaged his wounds,
pouring on oil and wine. Then he put
the man on his own donkey,
brought him to an inn and took care of him.

*35 The next day he took out two denarii and gave them
to the innkeeper. 'Look after him,'
he said, 'and when I return,
I will reimburse you for any extra expense you may have.'*

*36 "Which of these three do you think
was a neighbor to the man
who fell into the hands of robbers?"*

*37 The expert in the law replied, "The
one who had mercy on him."
Jesus told him, "Go and do likewise."*

The road from Jerusalem to Jericho was a rocky, dangerous road where thieves frequently attacked travelers, robbed them, and left them half dead. Perhaps Jesus and His disciples had gone down that road and knew its dangers. There were no modern, comfortable "rest stops" along the way. This sets the scene for the rest of the parable.

What the robbers did to the man is typical of the way robbers operate. Here is a man, lying on the side of that rocky road, almost dead from the beating they gave him, and along comes a priest. In a little while, along comes a Levite. Jesus does not tell us why the priest and the Levite both **passed by on the other side.** As God had arranged centuries before, Jewish priests all came from the tribe of Levi. It is easy to see that Jesus is subtly criticizing the behavior of the priest and the Levite.

To speculate about things not revealed in the Biblical text is not wise. Jesus knew there was no specific law requiring the priest or the Levite to help this dying man. The third person to come along was neither a priest nor a Levite. He was only a half-blood from the Jewish viewpoint, and they believed he had "no favor" in God's sight. The hatred some of the Jewish people had for the Samaritans had begun centuries before, and was still prevalent in the days of Jesus. *This hatred did not come from their law.* The fact that Jesus chose a despised Samaritan to be the true neighbor in this parable may have offended the lawyer, but it did not keep him from seeing that Jesus was teaching him about mercy. Jesus wants us to have mercy -- *even for a stranger.*

There are a few more thoughts we must consider from this parable. The first is the gentle care the Samaritan gave the injured man. Who this half-dead man was is not revealed. He was a human being who, without help, would have died on the side of a lonely, rocky road. What did the Samaritan do?

> **He took pity on him,**
> **he bandaged his wounds,**
> **he poured on oil and wine,**
> **he put the man on his own donkey,**
> **brought him to an inn,**
> **he took care of him,**
> **he paid the innkeeper to look after him and,**
> **he promised to reimburse the innkeeper**
> **for any extra expense.**

We know that the love of God lived in that man's heart, *and he was a Samaritan, of all things!* He did not begrudge anything he did for the wounded man. He did not hesitate to put him on his own donkey while he himself walked. He paid the lodging costs, and promised the innkeeper he would pay any additional expense incurred. This parable touches a sensitive spot in all of us. If these things impact us and touch our hearts, *then so did they impact the heart of the lawyer.* At the end of the parable, Jesus asked another question.

> **36 "Which of these three do you think**
> **was a neighbor to the man**
> **who fell into the hands of robbers?"**

Another thought: this parable **is not about** how much gratitude the injured man felt for the Samaritan. This parable is about **every believer** -- how **each one of us** helps those we find on the rocky roads of life. The reply of the expert in the law made no mention of the Samaritan, and some criticize him for that, but the lawyer recognized what the Samaritan did. He saw the mercy of God in the Samaritan's actions. He replied,

"The one who had mercy on him."

The joy of following Jesus is in doing good for others, as the Samaritan, even for someone we may not know at all. God wants His people to do good works at every opportunity we may have, seven days a week, twenty-four hours a day. How do we know? Jesus made it plain when He spoke those final victorious words to the lawyer.

"Go and do likewise."

Wow! What a challenge! Let us consider some lessons we can learn from this parable. First, nothing is known about the victim. Was he a Jew? An Egyptian? An Ethiopian? A priest or Levite? A Syrian? Did he have black hair? Or, was he a blond? Second, we have no mention, not one word, about his response to the Samaritan's care. In this parable, Jesus uttered nothing about how the injured man should respond.

Third, the question was, **Who is my neighbor?** Not, *How is the neighbor to respond when I do him good?* May God help us not inject into these parables some concept, or teaching, or direction, which Jesus did not include in what He did say. This principle applies to all the teachings and parables of Jesus.

Jesus won this victory without firing a shot. Oops! They did not have guns in those days. Jesus did this without rattling one saber, without throwing one spear, without using a single dagger to kill. And no blood was shed by anyone except the one beaten by the robbers. Perhaps the lawyer shed a few tears.

Jesus – 1; the Expert in the Law – 0

There were a few times when the adversaries of Jesus may have felt they were on the verge of accomplishing their long-held goal – the death of Jesus. Two "witnesses" distorted the words of Jesus concerning *the temple* into a very different, very damaging testimony (Matthew 26:59 – 66). **Caiaphas smelled the aroma of victory.** But Jesus remained silent until Caiaphas demanded a specific answer: *Tell us if you are the Christ, the Son of God.* Jesus said simply, *Yes, it is as you say.* Caiaphas exploded with rage, tearing his clothes and shouting, *Blasphemy!* All the leaders joined in the viciousness, and Jesus was spat upon, beaten, mocked, bound again, and sent to Pilate.

Pilate was not eager to condemn Jesus, but he could not withstand the unrelenting pressure from the Jewish leaders. In the presence of all the people, he washed his hands, symbolically denying any guilt for this travesty, stating, *I am innocent of this man's blood.* He handed Jesus over to the soldiers to be crucified. The smell of victory for Caiaphas was becoming stronger. But final victory must wait until Jesus was on a cross – dead. They had accomplished their goal, but there was not much time for them to celebrate their victory. A huge problem confronted them earlier in the morning of the third day – **the tomb of Jesus was empty.**

CHAPTER SIXTEEN

The Tomb of Jesus is Empty

Bailiff: *Please present your findings for*

The Sanhedrin's Failed Efforts to Keep the Tomb Secure

From the viewpoint of the Sanhedrin and other Jewish leaders, there was no possibility of a resurrection. What did they do?

The Sanhedrin's Problem:

Prevent the Theft of the Body of Jesus

Sundown ended the Jewish day, and probably *early* on the Sabbath Day, the chief priests and the Pharisees went to Pilate. To complicate matters, that particular Sabbath Day coincided with the Passover, a very important day for all Jewish people.

By setting a guard at the tomb, the Jewish leaders actually *made it more easily proved that Jesus actually was raised from the dead*. Had there been no guard at all, the claim that "his disciples came and stole the body away" would be more difficult for the disciples of Jesus to refute.

A "guard" is made up of a number of soldiers. Military protocol requires a "guard" to be comprised of as many soldiers as the task requires. To secure the entrance of the tomb, probably no more than four squads of four soldiers each were authorized by Pilate (See Acts 12:4). Under normal circumstances, this would be adequate coverage for the three days.

But who were these guards? Some say they were the Jewish Temple Guards, but Matthew states they were soldiers (Matthew 28:12). These guards were assigned by Pilate for temporary duty to guard the tomb under the guidance of the chief priests and elders. What began as an easy assignment on Saturday turned into a nightmare before dawn Sunday morning. The nightmare began with an earthquake which demanded the attention of everyone, including all of the soldiers.

They were so terror-stricken by what they saw, *they shook and became like dead men*. They had seen *some being* in brilliant white with lightning flashes all around come down from somewhere, roll the stone away from the tomb, then sit down on top of it. About that time, Mary Magdalene and the other women arrived and saw the angel sitting on that big stone.

After their frightening experience at the tomb, the soldiers saw the women enter the tomb, come back out, and rush away. Some of the soldiers then went to tell the chief priests what had happened. There are two reasons they did not report to Pilate: one, they had been put under the authority of the chief priests by Pilate; soldiers stay in the "chain of command." Second, they would not want to report an empty tomb to Pilate because it could mean the death penalty for dereliction of duty.

How did the chief priests handle this sensitive situation? Matthew's account answers the question quite clearly.

The evidence of the empty tomb cannot be refuted because everyone admitted that the body of Jesus was gone. The guards proclaimed it (Matt. 28:11 – 15); the women, including Mary Magdalene, announced it; both Peter and John saw it themselves. In addition, the chief priests bought the silence of the guards which further supports evidence of a miraculous event. That the tomb was empty cannot be disputed.

Even though there is no evidence that the guards ever looked into the empty tomb, there were several very reliable witnesses to the fact that the tomb was empty. It is important to read about their experiences.

o o o o o

Bailiff: *Please introduce the testimonies of*

The Living Witnesses to the Empty Tomb of Jesus

Several women had plans to use spices to complete the preparation of the body of Jesus for burial. They knew Joseph had not had time to do this before sundown, the beginning of the Sabbath. The tomb was already open when they arrived. There is no record of anyone, other than the soldiers, witnessing the angel moving the stone away from the tomb of Jesus.

When four persons write about the same event, each one will write about the more outstanding things from his own viewpoint. We know that sometimes a Biblical writer will focus on one person in an event and not mention others that may have been present. Keep this in mind any time you read the Gospels. The empty tomb is a "witness," but not one that speaks in a human voice.

o o o o o

Bailiff: *Please present the evidence for*

**Mary Magdalene and The other Women
Finding the Tomb Empty!**

We need to notice what happened before Jesus made Himself known to Mary Magdalene and the other women. The women had gone together to the tomb.

After the Sabbath was over at sundown on Saturday, the women prepared burial spices to take to the tomb. Early the next morning as they walked along, they wondered who would roll that huge stone away. When they arrived, the tomb was open, and they saw a powerful angel, with an appearance like lightning, sitting on that stone as if to defy the soldiers to enter the tomb. These guards had already been so frightened by the earthquake, and that bright angel, they looked like dead men (Matthew 28:2 – 4).

Did these women see the angel come down? No, for when they arrived, the stone was no longer blocking the entrance. Did they see the angel sitting on the stone? Yes. The angel comforted them and told them that Jesus had risen. He then told them to go into the tomb and see for themselves (v. 5 – 7).

Neither Matthew nor Mark records all the events that took place. Mark, in 16:8, Luke, in 24:1 – 8, and John, in 20:1 – 2, give additional details. These passages tell us how afraid and bewildered the women were, and that they ran back to report to Peter and the others. Mark reports they did not speak to anyone as they ran back. Fear had taken control of their hearts.

How would anyone, seeing these events, react to what they saw? The soldiers saw the angel roll the stone away. The women saw the bright angel sitting on the stone. Inside the open tomb, they saw two men in white robes who asked: *"Why do you look for the living among the dead? He is not here; he has risen!"* (Luke 24:5 – 6). They told them to tell His disciples. The disciples were dumbfounded. Peter and John ran to the tomb and were astonished by what they saw inside. They went back, Peter wondering, John believing. It is difficult to imagine how anyone would have reacted as a soldier, or one of the women, or as either Peter or John; *but in our hearts, we must see and believe these marvelous events!*

The details Mark recorded are strong evidence that Mary Magdalene and the women followed more slowly as Peter and John made their hurried race to the tomb.

o o o o o

Bailiff: *Please tell us about*

Peter and John Running to See the Empty Tomb

John 20:3 – 10

3 So Peter and the other disciple started for the tomb.

4 Both were running, but the other disciple outran Peter and reached the tomb first. 5 He bent over and looked in at the strips of linen lying there but did not go in.

6 Then Simon Peter came along behind him and went straight into the tomb. He saw the strips of linen lying there, 7 as well as the cloth that had been wrapped around Jesus' head. The cloth was still lying in its place, separate from the linen.

8 Finally the other disciple, who had reached the tomb first, also went inside. He saw and believed. 9 (They still did not understand from Scripture that Jesus had to rise from the dead.)

10 Then the disciples went back to where they were staying.

Peter, who entered the tomb quickly, was puzzled about the empty tomb with the grave clothes neatly in place. John entered, saw what Peter had seen, and believed. Then, they both returned to where they had been staying.

Everyone knew the tomb was empty. Everyone knew the body of Jesus was missing. At this point, who *did believe* Jesus had been raised from the dead? Not the women, because they told the disciples, *"They have taken the Lord out of the tomb, and we don't know where they have put him!"* Not the chief priests, because their main strategy had been to guard the tomb to prevent the disciples from stealing the body and claiming Jesus had been raised from death. Not Peter or John even though John believed *something,* but it was not that Jesus had been raised from the dead (v. 9). Not the disciples, because it took time to face the truth: *God had raised Jesus –* a concept foreign to human experience. And especially not Thomas – he was full of doubt.

Then, at the second appearance of Jesus to His disciples, Thomas saw Him, felt the nail prints, put his hand into His opened side, and proclaimed, *"My Lord and my God!"* They all knew – *Jesus was alive and standing in their presence!*

This is a Special Cloud – a silent Testimony – a very unusual victory, one no human being can achieve. Jesus won this Victory, not just over the Jewish leaders, but over Satan and all his powers, his dominion, all the rulers of darkness, death and hell. He won this victory by **offering Himself to God** *– for you, for everyone!* Jesus opened the door of forgiveness for all who come to Him in obedient faith.

Forgiveness by the Holy God of Heaven!
What a blessing this victory is! –
freely offered to all people.
The overwhelming testimony of the empty tomb –

the Risen Messiah, Jesus!

CLOUD SIX

That Great Cloud of Living
Witnesses of a Risen Messiah

CHAPTER SEVENTEEN

The Testimony of the Many
Living Witnesses

Judge: *You now have the task of presenting the actual people who saw Jesus after He was raised. Please give us an introductory outline, and I will have the Bailiff call for each event in proper order.*
Me: *Thank you, Your Honor.*

Brief Outline

The writers of the New Testament recorded **many** witnesses of the risen Jesus. Most of these events took place over a period of about forty days; but later Jesus also appeared to Saul of Tarsus, Ananias, and later again to the apostle John. The numerous scripture texts for the first four important witness groups or individuals will be given as they are presented.

First, Mary Magdalene, Mary, the mother
of James, Joanna, and Salome
Second, Cleopas and Simon
Third, Ten of the Eleven, Thomas not present
Fourth, All the Eleven including Thomas

The following is a list of the others to whom Jesus appeared, followed by the scripture reference.

Five hundred of the Brothers (I Corinthians 15:6)
James (I Corinthians 15:7)
Disciples at the Sea of Tiberias (John 21:1 – 14)
Teaching the Apostles over 40 days (Acts 1:2 – 3)
The Apostles witnessing Jesus Ascending
into Heaven (Acts 1:4 – 9)
Saul of Tarsus (Acts 9)
Ananias (Acts 9)
The Apostle John on the Isle of Patmos
(Revelation, especially chapters 1 – 3)

o o o o o

Bailiff: *Please present the account of*

Jesus Appearing to Mary Magdalene and the Other Women

We have read the account of these women and know of their frightening experiences at the empty tomb. They hurried to find the disciples and report the angels' announcement that Jesus had been raised from the grave. Peter and John ran to the tomb, saw it empty, then returned to where they had been staying. Up to this point, Jesus had not been seen by anyone.

In the meantime, what did the women do? *The scripture does not say but it can be reasoned out very easily.* The women had obviously returned to the tomb as Peter and John were running to it. Let the scriptures speak.

John 20:10 – 18

10 Then the disciples went back to where they were staying.

*11 Now Mary stood outside the
tomb crying. As she wept,
she bent over to look into the tomb
12 and saw two angels
in white, seated where Jesus' body had been,
one at the head and the other at the foot.*

This is the evidence that the women went back to the tomb, arriving after Peter and John. How can we know this? In verse 11 above, the word "***Now***" takes us back to the women, *who also had to be at the tomb as Peter and John came out and left.* The magnitude of the situation – *the empty tomb and the missing body* – was so great there was no time for conversation. It was the angels who asked Mary a question.

*13 They asked her, "Woman, why are
you crying?" "They have
taken my Lord away," she said,
"and I don't know where they have put him."*

*14 At this, she turned around and saw Jesus
standing there, but she did not realize that it was Jesus.*

Still very distraught, Mary answered, "***They have taken my Lord away,***" and, "***I don't know where they have put him.***" At this point, we can be sure that Mary, and *all* the women, *knew that the tomb was empty.* Did they believe Jesus had been raised from death? Not at this point; they still wanted to find His body and anoint it with the burial ointments. When Mary first saw someone just outside the tomb, she did not recognize who it was. But then she heard the voice asking why she was crying.

*15 He asked her, "Woman, why are
you crying? Who is it you are*

*looking for?" Thinking he was the
gardener, she said, "Sir,
if you have carried him away, tell me
where you have put him,
and I will get him."*

The women were still looking for the body of Jesus. The tomb was empty, but they still had no idea that Jesus had been raised from death to life.

*16 Jesus said to her, "Mary."
She turned toward him and cried out in Aramaic,
"Rabboni!" (which means "Teacher").*

*17 Jesus said, "Do not hold on to me,
for I have not yet ascended
to the Father. Go instead to my brothers and tell them,
'I am ascending to my Father and your
Father, to my God and your God.'"*

*18 Mary Magdalene went to the disciples
with the news: "I have seen
the Lord!" And she told them that he
had said these things to her.*

When Jesus called her name, she immediately recognized His voice and called him *"Teacher!"* She was the first to be able to believe because she had seen and even talked to the **risen Jesus**.

Were the other women still with her? Matthew's account does not mention Mary, only "the women." Perhaps Jesus spoke to Mary first, and when Mary cried out *"Teacher!"* they all came to bow down at His feet. They then had another message for the disciples: "*We have seen the risen Lord, Jesus!"* (Notice: *We* is plural, **so must include the women.**)

Remember, this all happened on the morning of the first day of the week, *the Resurrection Morning!*

After the angels gave the women the message to tell the disciples and the other believers, their encounter with Jesus took place. Matthew tells another part of it.

Matthew 28:8 – 10

8 So the women hurried away from the
tomb, afraid yet filled with joy,
and ran to tell his disciples.

9 Suddenly Jesus met them. "Greetings,"
he said. They came to him,
clasped his feet and worshiped him.

10 Then Jesus said to them, "Do not be afraid.
Go and tell my brothers to go to Galilee;
there they will see me."

Again, the women ran to tell the brothers and sisters; this time they had a more amazing experience to report – **they had seen and talked with the risen Jesus!**

o o o o o

Bailiff: *Please present the unusual way*

Jesus Identified Himself to Cleopas and Simon

Cleopas and Simon (not Simon Peter), some time early Sunday morning, were walking to Emmaus, about seven miles from Jerusalem. They were talking about the tragic event that had taken place two days before. They were further baffled by the reports of the women that the tomb was empty; Jesus' body was not there; and this was confirmed by Peter and John who had quickly run to the tomb to see for themselves.

While they were walking and talking, a "stranger" joined them and began to walk with them, but it was quite some time before Jesus allowed them to know who He was.

He asked them, *"What are you discussing together as you walk along?"* (Luke 24:17). They were surprised that anyone could have been in Jerusalem and not know *the things* that had happened. so they asked this "visitor to Jerusalem" how he did not know. *"What things?"* he asked.

They told this "strange visitor" about Jesus who was *a prophet, powerful in word and deed before God and all the people* (v. 19b). They spoke freely of their belief, and that of the people, that Jesus was the one they had been waiting for. They spoke about their hope, that He *. . . was the one who was going to redeem Israel.* Their hopes were shattered when their chief priests and rulers turned him over to the Romans to be crucified.

They had more to tell this stranger. Evidently, Cleopas and Simon were a part of the 120 disciples who had gathered with the apostles in Jerusalem over the Passover weekend. They told Him that some women had found the tomb empty, and reported seeing a vision of angels. They said the angels told them Jesus had risen. They also told about their companions who went to the tomb and found it just as the women had said. These witnesses testified that the tomb no longer contained the body of Jesus (Luke 24:17 – 24). We know that at that time none of them had seen Jesus, or His body.

This walking companion of Cleopas and Simon began to speak to them. What He said in the beginning is very significant for us to understand and use today. We need this understanding as we carry out our service to God in today's very unstable world.

Luke 24:25 – 26

25 He said to them, "How foolish you are,
and how slow to believe all that the
prophets have spoken!

26 Did not the Messiah have to suffer these things
and then enter his glory?"

Jesus told them **how foolish** they had been, **and how slow to believe all that the prophets have spoken!** He then implied that they should have known that **the Messiah** (would) **have to suffer these things.** We have already presented much of what the prophet Isaiah said about the suffering of the Messiah, *and that is what the chief priests and rulers of Israel had missed!* We need to stand in awe of these prophets and their words. It is not just one prophet with one message, it is many prophets with many messages **that all point to the One Messiah.** *It is urgent to grasp the accuracy of the words of these prophets.*

For example, if a man says, *"It is going to rain tomorrow,"* no one would bat an eye. In fact, a few people might go outside carrying an umbrella. But if he says, *"Tomorrow, at 2:14 P.M., lightning will strike a huge pine tree in the back southwestern corner of my neighbor's yard, split the tree in two, with half falling in my yard and half falling in his yard,"* that is a very different prediction. There are many specific details with no room for excuses if there is any variation. If the sun is shining all afternoon on the predicted day, then you would know that man is a false prophet!

We have not tried to write about **all** the Old Testament prophets and their words; there are just too many. There are many specifics, predicted over hundreds of years, concerning the Messiah to come. However, there is no person in all of history who fulfills more than a few of these clear predictions – **to the contrary, Jesus fulfilled the specifics of all these prophecies**.

Jesus had not yet made Himself known to Cleopas and Simon when He began speaking about Moses, then the prophets, and *explained to them what was said in all the Scriptures concerning Himself* (v. 27b). We do not know how far out of Jerusalem they were when Jesus joined them, but He used that time to tell them about those men of God who prophesied the details of the coming Messiah.

They arrived at their destination and insisted that this knowledgeable stranger stay with them; nighttime was coming soon. They prepared an evening meal and their guest took the bread, gave thanks, and served them. At this, their eyes were opened and they realized that it was Jesus – *then He vanished from their sight* (v. 30, 31).

Cleopas and Simon immediately returned to Jerusalem, found the apostles and those assembled with them, and recited their experience, saying, *"It is true! The Lord has risen and has appeared to Simon."* Simon and Cleopas were additional eye-witnesses *to the resurrection of Jesus, the Christ, the Son of God!*

o o o o o

Bailiff: *Please present the account of*

**Jesus' First Appearance to the
Disciples – Thomas not Present**

While these two men from Emmaus were reporting this amazing event to the Eleven, Jesus appeared to them all. He comforted them, saying, *"Peace be with you."* (Luke 24:36). It is difficult to wear the sandals of those who were together with the apostles, listening to Cleopas and Simon when, all of a sudden, *Jesus is standing in their midst.* Some thought they were seeing a ghost (a disembodied spirit), were startled and afraid, but Jesus quickly asked, *"Why are you troubled, and why do doubts rise in your minds?"* (v. 38).

230

While He was still with them, He had told them that He must die at the hands of cruel men, but to take heart, on the third day He would rise again – but for them, that was ancient history. It is not so much as they had forgotten, it is more the power of the traditional **misinformation** they had all heard about the Messiah, *and their vision of the Messiah driving the Romans back to Rome.* **Jesus did not fit that mold!**

Understanding their dilemma, He quickly told them to, *"Look at my hands and my feet. It is I myself! Touch me and see; a ghost does not have flesh and bones, as you see I have."* (v. 39). Jesus then showed them His hands and His feet. He asked for something to eat; they gave Him a piece of broiled fish. He took it and ate it in their presence. Jesus patiently explained, and *had them examine the proof!*

o o o o o

Bailiff: *Please present the account of*

**Jesus Appearing to All Eleven
Apostles, including Thomas**

John 20:24 – 29

*24 Now Thomas (also known as
Didymus), one of the Twelve,
was not with the disciples when Jesus came.
25 So the other disciples told him,
"We have seen the Lord!"
But he said to them, "Unless I see
the nail marks in his hands
and put my finger where the nails were,
and put my hand into his side, I will not believe."*

26 A week later his disciples were in the house again, and Thomas was with them. Though the doors were locked, Jesus came and stood among them and said, "Peace be with you!"

27 Then he said to Thomas, "Put your finger here; see my hands. Reach out your hand and put it into my side. Stop doubting and believe."

28 Thomas said to him, "My Lord and my God!"

29 Then Jesus told him, "Because you have seen me, you have believed; blessed are those who have not seen and yet have believed."

Jesus understood that Thomas had a problem comprehending the reality of His resurrection. It contravenes all human experience. And Jesus understands that we also have that same problem. However, the evidence presented by *That Great Cloud of Living Witnesses of the Risen Messiah, the Lord Jesus,* gives solid and strong *reasons to believe.* These eye-witnesses provide confidence and strength to our faith, and we are grateful.

Jesus chose the Twelve from ordinary people, fishermen, tax collectors, etc. He, Himself, worked with Joseph as a carpenter. From His teachings about flocks and herds, harvest time, and vineyards, we can imagine that Jesus probably had a farmer or two among His apostles. *They were all trained by Jesus to be the kind of people anyone could trust.*

The only exception was Judas, a thief and betrayer, who, in deep remorse, killed himself before Jesus died. He was not a witness of the resurrection. The *Cloud of very much alive Witnesses* gives us confidence in the resurrection of

Jesus. The New Testament accurately records the fulfillment of the prophecies concerning these events. The testimony of the apostles of Jesus is that of honest people, who gave their lives rather than deny this great truth.

oooooo

Bailiff: *Please present the record of Jesus' appearance to*

The More than Five Hundred and James

The Apostle Paul gave a brief summary of the appearances of Jesus after His resurrection; these are not in chronological order. This first one, the *Five Hundred,* is not recorded by any other New Testament writer, nor do we know when it happened. Paul acknowledges that Jesus appeared to them at the same time, but that it was so long ago some had already passed away (1 Corinthians 15:6).

When Jesus appeared to James is not recorded (15:7). After Jesus was born, Joseph and Mary had four other sons and some daughters; James was one of the younger brothers of Jesus. James later became an elder in Jerusalem and wrote the Book of James.

Did Jesus also appear to Jude, another of His brothers, who wrote the New Testament Book that bears his name? It must have been difficult for James and Jude to realize that their older brother, Jesus, was truly the Messiah. We know that while Jesus was still in Galilee, his brothers had not yet come to believe (John 7:1 – 5). However, the writings of both men reveal a fervent faith in their older brother, Jesus.

James, as an elder in Jerusalem, showed a clear understanding of how to solve a difficult problem among believers. See Acts, chapter 15, and learn how he resolved a severe conflict in viewpoints. The evils Jude identified in his world are the same evils enslaving people today. Both brothers proclaim that God, through Jesus Christ, is the only answer, the only hope.

o o o o o

Bailiff: *Please present the record of*

Jesus Appearing to Peter and Other Disciples at the Sea of Galilee

Peter, with Thomas, Nathanael, James, John, and two other disciples, got in a boat to catch fish from the Sea of Galilee. They fished all night and still had empty nets. Early the next morning, they heard a voice from the shore asking if they had caught anything. They answered honestly, *"No."* The voice called back for them to cast their nets on the right side of the boat and *you will find some* (v. 6). They did and the nets began to fill with large fish, so many they could not haul the catch into the boat; they had to pull it to the shore, about a hundred yards away. This event is recorded in John 21:1 – 14.

John, the observant one, was the first to realize that the man on the shore was Jesus. He said to Peter, *"It is the Lord!"* Peter. still quick to act, put his outer garment on, jumped into the water, and swam to shore, leaving the others to haul the heavy nets to shore. They all then realized it was *Jesus on the shore, alive and fixing breakfast for them!* On the shore, coals of fire were cooking fish, and there was bread.

Jesus told them to bring some of the fish they had just caught. It was Peter who got back into the boat, dragged the net to shore, and let Jesus complete preparing their breakfast.

Not one of these disciples had to be told that the man on the shore was Jesus; they all knew. During this third appearance of Jesus to His disciples, they heard Him tell them where the fish were; they knew the catch of 153 large fish would break most nets. By the time they saw the breakfast He had prepared, they already knew it was Jesus.

We do not know why Peter went back to fishing. Was it because of despair? No! Why were they in Galilee? What message from the angels at the tomb had the women rushed to tell the disciples? Mark quotes the angel instructing the women to go tell the disciples and Peter that Jesus would meet them in Galilee (Mark 16:6 – 7).

No Master Sergeant, or Chief Petty Officer, ever had the ability to train recruits like Jesus trained His disciples, especially those chosen to be His Apostles. They witnessed the compassionate heart of Jesus as He healed the sick, restored sight to the blind and hearing to the deaf, raised the dead, calmed violent winds and monstrous waves, walked on the Sea of Galilee, and called Lazarus to come out from his four-day stay in a tomb. These courageous men and women saw God working through Jesus, time and time again. All the world needs to hear their absolutely awesome message –

the crucified Jesus has been raised
from death and is alive!

o o o o o

Bailiff: *Please present the record*
where Jesus spent forty days

Giving His Apostles Proof of His Resurrection, and Teaching His Apostles about the Kingdom of God

Acts 1:1 – 3

1 In my former book, Theophilus, I
wrote about all that Jesus began
to do and to teach 2 until the day he was taken

up to heaven, after giving instructions
through the Holy Spirit
to the apostles he had chosen.

3 After his suffering, he presented himself to them
and gave many convincing proofs that
he was alive. He appeared
to them over a period of forty days and
spoke about the kingdom of God.

What instructions did Jesus give to His Apostles? Two important things He taught them are mentioned.

One, **undeniable proof that he had been raised from the dead.**

Two, **instructions about the Kingdom of God.**

This again is important information all believers need to follow today; our task is to share the Gospel with those still in darkness. The witnesses of His resurrection have given us compelling evidence that Jesus is alive. What Jesus taught His apostles about the Kingdom of God during those forty days was not revealed. However, there is a way to learn – **study what these apostles <u>did</u>** after Jesus filled them with God's Holy Spirit. **What they did was what Jesus had taught them to do.**

They fearlessly proclaimed the Gospel to thousands on the Day of Pentecost, then gradually spread out to many parts of the world. They began the task of telling all people on earth about the **blessed Light of the World, JESUS! Our task is to Reflect that Light; share that Truth Message – until everyone everywhere knows Jesus!**

o o o o o

Bailiff: *Please present the record of*

The Witnesses Who Saw Jesus Ascend into Heaven

It is good to keep in mind the events leading up to the ascension of Jesus. After the forty days of proving He was truly alive and teaching them more about His Kingdom, several events occurred. First, they were eating together when Jesus gave them a command and a promise. The command was for them to wait in Jerusalem, and the promise was that God would fill them with the Holy Spirit (Acts 1:1 – 5).

Second, at a later meeting, the disciples asked a question which revealed how deeply some traditions were ingrained in Jewish minds. Even His apostles still thought that the Messiah was going to *restore the kingdom to Israel!* Jesus answered by telling them God was in control of such things; He then told them what their responsibilities would be.

Acts 1:6 – 8

6 Then they gathered around him and asked him,
"Lord, are you at this time
going to restore the kingdom to Israel?"

7 He said to them: "It is not for you to know the times
or dates the Father has set by his own authority.

8 But you will receive power when
the Holy Spirit comes on you;
and you will be my witnesses in
Jerusalem, and in all Judea
and Samaria, and to the ends of the earth."

Jesus did not belittle His apostles for asking the question; neither did He try to do more teaching. His focus was on the main purpose these men would be charged to carry out – *be His witnesses in Jerusalem, Judea, Samaria, then to the very ends of the earth.* The Holy Spirit would give them the power to do what Jesus wanted them to do. Almost immediately after Jesus spoke those words – *he was taken up before their very eyes, and a cloud hid him from their sight* (Acts 1:9).

They waited about ten days; the promise of Jesus was fulfilled. The Holy Spirit fell on the apostles and they began the task Jesus had given them. Several thousand people heard Peter and the apostles speaking to them, not with a Galilean dialect, but *in their own native languages!* They were seeing and hearing the power of the Holy Spirit in these twelve men from Galilee.

There are two other amazing appearances of Jesus which Luke describes in detail beginning in Acts 9.

o o o o o

Bailiff: *Please present the account of Jesus appearing to*

Saul of Tarsus, an Enemy
and
Ananias, a Trusting Disciple

We would never choose an enemy, a dedicated and vicious enemy, to "join our team." But God is able to look into the hearts of people and see what is truly inside. *No human being, not one, can do this!* Saul, by relentless, determined efforts to destroy what Christians were doing, viciously persecuted the followers of Jesus *because he was sure that was what God wanted him to do!* Several years after He had ascended into heaven, Jesus confronted Saul on the road to Damascus in Syria. Notice the straightforward manner Jesus used with both Saul and Ananias.

238

Acts 9:1 – 19

1 Meanwhile, Saul was still breathing
out murderous threats
against the Lord's disciples. He went to the high priest
2 and asked him for letters to the
synagogues in Damascus,
so that if he found any there who belonged to the Way,
whether men or women, he might take
them as prisoners to Jerusalem.

3 As he neared Damascus on his
journey, suddenly a light
from heaven flashed around him. 4 He fell to the ground
and heard a voice say to him,
"Saul, Saul, why do you persecute me?"

5 "Who are you, Lord?" Saul asked.
"I am Jesus, whom you are persecuting," he replied.
6 "Now get up and go into the city,
and you will be told what you must do."

The brilliance of the light reminds us of the angel that rolled away the stone, and the two angels inside the tomb. Saul could not handle that much light, so did not see Jesus, but immediately after Jesus said, *"I am Jesus, whom you are persecuting,"* he knew it was Jesus. The Lord did not discuss anything with Saul, not even his record of persecutions or murderous threats, He just told Saul, *"Now get up and go into the city, and you will be told what you must do."*

Jesus did not tell Saul to destroy those papers from the High Priest, or to repent of his sins against His followers. Jesus told him to *go and wait* for someone else, not Jesus, to tell him what he **must do**.

What about the others traveling with Saul? How did they respond? Let us continue reading from Acts 9.

7 The men traveling with Saul stood there speechless; they heard the sound but did not see anyone.

8 Saul got up from the ground, but when he opened his eyes he could see nothing. So they led him by the hand into Damascus. 9 For three days he was blind, and did not eat or drink anything.

The companions of Saul led him into Damascus, evidently to the very house of Judas on Straight Street. Luke continues the story which includes how Ananias became involved.

10 In Damascus there was a disciple named Ananias. The Lord called to him in a vision, "Ananias!" "Yes, Lord," he answered.

11 The Lord told him, "Go to the house of Judas on Straight Street and ask for a man from Tarsus named Saul, for he is praying.

12 In a vision he has seen a man named Ananias come and place his hands on him to restore his sight."

Ananias, a true disciple to whom Jesus appeared in a vision, was also a normal human being. The instructions Jesus gave Ananias were clear and simple. Go to the house of Judas and put your hands on a man (What's his name?), and restore his sight. Sounds simple enough but Ananias was shocked when he heard the name of the "blind" man: *Saul, of Tarsus!* The word about Saul had gotten to Damascus and Ananias was confused. He knew Jesus was talking to him, **but ? ? ?**

If this were not such a serious matter, it might be laughable. Think about it: Ananias was sure that *Jesus* had appeared to him – *Jesus*, raised from the dead; *Jesus,* who ascended on high; *Jesus,* who healed all kinds of illnesses; *Jesus, the Son of God! How could He **not know** what kind of person this Saul of Tarsus was?* So, Ananias felt compelled to tell Jesus – *something He did not know?*

> **13 "Lord," Ananias answered, "I have
> heard many reports about
> this man and all the harm he has
> done to your holy people
> in Jerusalem. 14 And he has come
> here with authority from the
> chief priests to arrest all who call on your name."**

> **15 But the Lord said to Ananias,
> "Go! This man is my chosen
> instrument to proclaim my name to the Gentiles
> and their kings and to the people of Israel.**

> **16 I will show him how much he
> must suffer for my name."**

How would we react to Jesus if He appeared to us and told us to go to Chicago and confront that city's most powerful gangster? Would we, as Ananias did, wonder if Jesus really understood who that criminal was? How could we possibly think that *we* could tell Jesus *something He did not know!* Ananias was courageous because he trusted Jesus enough to do what Jesus commanded.

241

17 Then Ananias went to the house and entered it. Placing his hands on Saul, he said, "Brother Saul, the Lord—Jesus, who appeared to you on the road as you were coming here—has sent me so that you may see again and be filled with the Holy Spirit."
18 Immediately, something like scales fell from Saul's eyes, and he could see again. He got up and was baptized, 19 and after taking some food, he regained his strength.

Luke, in this first account, did not reveal who commanded Saul to be baptized. Years later, Paul, the Apostle, revealed that it was Ananias who asked him, **What are you waiting for? Get up, be baptized and wash your sins away, calling on His name.** This should be a strong warning to anyone who feels, thinks, or teaches that baptism is not important and essential. Saul had to put his old life of sin to death and bury it in water.

Years later, when he was attacked by a crowd of Jews in Jerusalem, Paul again told about this amazing experience on the road to Damascus,. We shall read the part that concerns both Saul and Ananias.

Acts 22:12 – 16

12 "A man named Ananias came to see me. He was a devout observer of the law and highly respected by all the Jews living there.

13 He stood beside me and said, "Brother Saul, receive your sight!" And at that very moment I was able to see him.

14 "Then he said: 'The God of our ancestors has chosen you

to know his will and to see the
Righteous One and to hear
words from his mouth. 15 You will
be his witness to all people
of what you have seen and heard.

16 And now what are you waiting
for? Get up, be baptized
and wash your sins away, calling on his name.'"

Paul, long after becoming an apostle, related more of the details of his encounter with Ananias. *You will be his witness to all people of what you have seen and heard.* How could he be a witness like the other apostles? Ananias answered the "how" when he said:

"The God of our ancestors has chosen you to know his will and to see the Righteous One and to hear words from his mouth." In other words, Jesus would continue to speak to him and guide him in all that He wanted him to do. Paul also became another **very live witness of the risen Jesus.**

Ananias also was a witness to the resurrection of Jesus. The Lord had appeared to him in a vision and told him how to help Saul. Before we leave Saul and Ananias, we need to see just a little more as Paul, as an apostle, recounts the same event before King Agrippa.

Acts 26:12 – 18

12 "On one of these journeys I was
going to Damascus with the
authority and commission of the
chief priests. 13 About noon,
King Agrippa, as I was on the road,
I saw a light from heaven,

*brighter than the sun, blazing around
me and my companions.
14 We all fell to the ground, and I
heard a voice saying to me
in Aramaic, 'Saul, Saul, why do you persecute me?
It is hard for you to kick against the goads.'*

*15 "Then I asked, 'Who are you, Lord?'
"'I am Jesus, whom you are
persecuting,' the Lord replied.*

*16 'Now get up and stand on your
feet. I have appeared to you
to appoint you as a servant and as a witness
of what you have seen and will see of me.*

*17 I will rescue you from your own people
and from the Gentiles. I am sending you to them*

*18 to open their eyes and turn them
from darkness to light,
and from the power of Satan to God,
so that they may receive forgiveness of sins and a place
among those who are sanctified by faith in me.'"*

Jesus did not pull any punches when He spoke to Saul. He told him he would be both a servant and a witness. He promised to rescue Saul from both Jews and Gentiles who would attack him physically and verbally. He did not tell him that he would become an apostle with the same status as Peter and the other apostles. It was Barnabas who went to Tarsus, found Saul, and brought him to Antioch to begin that ministry for Jesus.

Neither Saul nor Ananias had the day-to-day training Jesus had given the other apostles; yet Jesus picked those two, Saul and Ananias, from thousands of others to do what He knew they were capable of doing. *Our God is an awesome God!*

o o o o o

Bailiff: *Please relate how Jesus appeared to John in*

The Revelation

How Jesus appeared to John, as recorded in the Book of Revelation, is very different from His other appearances. Many scholars believe John did most if not all of his writing late in his life. The persecution of Christians under Domitian, Caesar, was severe throughout the Roman Empire. The theme of the Book of Revelation identifies the kind of suffering Christians had to endure in many parts of the Roman Empire under Domitian.

Revelation 1:1 – 2

1 The revelation from Jesus Christ,
which God gave him to show
his servants what must soon take place.
He made it known by sending his
angel to his servant John,
2 who testifies to everything he saw—that is,
the word of God and the testimony of Jesus Christ.

John is to write what he saw, and all of it from the Word of God. He will also give *the testimony of Jesus Christ.* Our task is to recognize that the revelation to John is part of the **Cloud of Living Witnesses to the Resurrection of Jesus.**

John was told to write a letter to the angel of each congregation in seven cities. This was truly a special experience for John. He had seen the *Risen Christ* in His crucified body, as had the other witnesses; but in the Revelation, John saw

Jesus in His glory. What John wrote to each congregation of believers in Jesus reveals human nature accurately, especially for our weaknesses. The letters urge faithfulness as long as we live, and good things are promised for those who overcome. To every congregation, each Christian is expected to be involved in the struggle to overcome. The essence of these letters is found throughout the teachings of Jesus.

Revelation 1:9 – 18

9 I, John, your brother and companion
in the suffering and kingdom
and patient endurance that are ours in Jesus,
was on the island of Patmos because of the word of God
and the testimony of Jesus.

10 On the Lord's Day I was in the Spirit,
and I heard behind me a loud voice like a trumpet,
11 which said: "Write on a scroll
what you see and send it
to the seven churches: to Ephesus, Smyrna, Pergamum,
Thyatira, Sardis, Philadelphia and Laodicea."

12 I turned around to see the voice
that was speaking to me.
And when I turned I saw seven golden lamp stands,
13 and among the lamp stands was
someone like a son of man,
dressed in a robe reaching down to his feet and
with a golden sash around his chest.

14 The hair on his head was white like wool,
as white as snow, and his eyes were like blazing fire.
15 His feet were like bronze glowing in a furnace,
and his voice was like the sound of rushing waters.

16 In his right hand he held seven stars, and coming
out of his mouth was a sharp, double-edged sword.
His face was like the sun shining in all its brilliance.

17 When I saw him, I fell at his feet
as though dead. Then he
placed his right hand on me and said: "Do not be afraid.
I am the First and the Last. 18 I am
the Living One; I was dead,
and now look, I am alive for ever and ever!
And I hold the keys of death and Hades.

John gave his **testimony of Jesus,** always from the word of God. It is believed that he was banished to the Isle of Patmos because he gave his testimony so fervently.

When John heard a voice and turned to see who had spoken to him, he saw **someone like a son of man.** Who was this? **This was Jesus in His glory!** How do we know? We know it was Jesus because of the very encouraging words He spoke to John.

17 . . . "Do not be afraid. I am the First and the Last.
18 I am the Living One; I was dead, and now look,
I am alive for ever and ever! And I hold
the keys of death and Hades."

Only Jesus has conquered death and Hades. He is the only **Living One,** who could say, *"I was dead, and now look, I am alive for ever and ever!"*

It is urgent that we understand why **Jesus, *the Messiah*, had to die.** In both the Old and New Covenants, we read of a few people who were raised from death, but unlike Jesus, they died again. By dying on this earth, Jesus showed His power over death. He lived in a body as human as ours, showing all of us that sin and evil and death could be defeated. Without

His death, there could be no resurrection to life, to life eternal for the faithful in Christ Jesus. By His sacrificial death, **He demonstrated, not only his power over death, but also His infinite love for all of us.**

All those who saw Jesus alive, after He was crucified, form another **Great Cloud of Witnesses.** All of them were alive; they saw Jesus, talked with Him, ate with Him, and bowed before Him: **Jesus, Christ, Messiah, Risen Lord!**

The testimony of these many witnesses is our evidence. Because of their faith in the truth of the *death and resurrection of Jesus,* many of them suffered severe persecutions, *yet they remained faithful!* Every witness, every testimony, every fulfilled prophecy proclaims loudly and clearly: **All of this is the work of a loving Father in Heaven. His heart full of love had to act to bring lost mankind out of the depths of evil, out of the deception of sin and death, out of hopeless despair, and into the clear, bright, constant Son Light of Jesus.**

That love brought Jesus to proclaim to all, just as He proclaimed to the believers in Laodicea (Revelation 3:19 – 22), that He is at our door, knocking, and He wants us to open the door and **let Him come in and share a meal with us.** Jesus is calling for people to leave the old life and its destructive ways, to allow Him to make us over into His image. He desires *to make us into living stones* and *use us to build that Holy Temple in which God lives by His Spirit.*

As we move closer to God day-by-day, we will also draw closer to one another *in Christ Jesus,* a powerful blessing. We will become *His living stones!* This is what these witnesses have shared with us – **God is calling! Jesus is calling! *We respond by***

keeping our eyes fixed on Jesus.

EPILOGUE

We have read about these great witnesses in Hebrews 11, observed the words of the prophets of Israel, and the prophets of the Messiah, to see clear evidences that they all spoke the truth from God. We have read the record of Jesus as He demonstrated His complete trust in God. Attacked by Satan himself, as well as by the Pharisees and other adversaries, He victoriously overcame every temptation of Satan and man. In all of this, He never did physical harm to anyone. He never drew a sword, never cast a spear, never lashed out in anger. He won every victory without shedding blood, until His very last victory over sin and death, ***and the blood shed was His own!***

We know there was no dead body to be found, and the testimony of the empty tomb is definite: ***Jesus is alive, He has conquered sin and death!*** We have walked with those who walked with Jesus, ate with Him, listened to Him, talked with Him, and were taught by Him. They *knew* Jesus had been raised from death, and was alive. Many of them were killed because ***they would not deny this truth.***

Our faith grew stronger in the research that led to the writing of this book, and we pray that yours has become stronger also. Other family members, friends, neighbors, and whomever God places before you are your opportunity to allow these clouds of witnesses to speak to them, increase their faith, and for some, perhaps *bring them* to faith. There is no better way to please God and honor Jesus who died for us all, than to

share this Good News with those you know and love.

ACKNOWLEDGEMENTS

Jeannine and I both owe a great debt of gratitude to many people. This includes our parents, fellow teachers, fellow missionaries, and many others over the last seventy plus years of our marriage. The spiritual influence of godly men and women early in our marriage helped us establish a strong foundation for our marriage and everything else in our lives. In Christian education, we remember Dr. Lacy Elrod and his wife Lucy, Dr. E. H. Ijams and his wife, Uma, all of whom set a high standard for both our teaching and our daily Christian lives. Fellow missionary families have been not only great co-workers, but also are long-lasting friends. They include: Roy and Joyce Mullinax, Edward and Sharon Short, Bob and Doris Frazier, Dr. Richard N. and Maudine Ady, George and Ruth Moore, Al and Sharon Henderson, John and Donna Camp, David and Vicky Finch, Eugene and Gretchen Brzozowski. A host of Chinese brothers and sisters in the Lord, who now live all over the world, have also been, and continue to be, encouragers and beloved friends, some for more than sixty years.

The production of *Gathering the Clouds* became possible because so many people helped, *more than fifty!* We have been told it is dangerous to list the names of helpers because, with the frailty of human memory, some names may be omitted. This is especially true for those who made valuable oral suggestions. In spite of the danger, we are printing out that list. We are taking the risk because we know all who helped are dear Christian friends who made their suggestions sincerely and respectfully. We ask forgiveness if we have omitted anyone's name – and we know they will grant it. That is the way it is when the love of the Lord lives in human hearts.

We did not begin the research for the purpose of writing a book. The texts that emerged just kept drawing us toward an examination of all the witnesses. This book has been through five major revisions, all of which brought a better final, readable text. We owe much to Dr. Sheila Vamplin, Dr. Don Kinder, Ronn and Susan Rubio, and many members of our FaithWalk Bible class who encouraged us to continue writing. Edward Short, co-worker for over fifty years and very close friend, has been a constant source of encouragement to us in many ways, including the writing of *Gathering the Clouds.*

The opportunity to teach many parts of the book to the FaithWalk class members brought many more suggestions. This led to asking class members, other friends and family to edit one or more chapters. The result was that each chapter had at least two editor/readers. Every suggestion had merit and most resulted in changes in the text.

Writing and publishing today has many challenges that typesetters of our Chinese booklets long ago could not dream of. We are deeply indebted to Kok Hai Tan for his always being available to keep our computers operating properly. Others who have given much guidance on computer use include our daughter, Diane T. Johnson, who also designed the front cover, Edward Short, and two large computer screens which enable us to read what we write as we write.

Included in the following list are homemakers, teachers, seminary professors, a prison inmate, nurses, a civil court judge, a college student, a retired university professor, and a businessman. They are listed in no certain order, and we pray that we have not overlooked any of --

Our Beloved Editor/Readers:

Jackie Williams, Ronn and Susan Rubio,
Brent and Deborah Mason,
Terrence Thomas, Don Meredith, Chris
Jones, Cindy Lawrence,
Steve Townsdin, J.D., Dr. Don and
Vicki Kinder, Edward Short,
Dr. Philip Slate, Don Morris, Caleb Cranford,
Don and Diane T. Johnson,
Steve and Ellen Thweatt, Gary and Telia
T. Galloway, Bruce Thweatt,
Jon and Sara Grizzle, Sean Thweatt, Ed and Pam Mosby,
Tony Forrest, Jeff and Barbara Sanders, Paula T. Hughes,
Bud and Julie T. Henry, and Dr. Mack and Sandra Thweatt.

We express our sincere gratitude to them, but the true glory belongs to God. All the good things mentioned here have come because the love of Jesus lives deep in the hearts of every one of our "editors" and encouragers. We also sincerely appreciate Sarah Turner, who served as our Concierge to guide us through the publishing process at LifeRich Publishing.

The authors are fully responsible for any errors in the contents of this book.

Enoch B. Thweatt, Jr. and Jeannine P. Thweatt

ABOUT THE AUTHORS

Enoch B. Thweatt, Jr. and Jeannine P. Thweatt, both in their nineties, were born in Nashville, Tennessee, and attended public schools. He served in the U.S. Navy in WWII, 1944 – 46. They married in 1948, have seven children, all of whom graduated from Taipei American High School in Taiwan. Enoch: B.A. 1950, Vanderbilt, Business Adm,, with Mathematics teaching credentials; M.A. 1956, Peabody College, School Adm.; MTh, 1979, Harding School of Theology (HST), Biblical Studies.

Jeannine: two quarters at David Lipscomb College (now University). When her mother was diagnosed with pancreatic cancer, Jeannine took care of her until her death in 1947. She later studied Chinese at Soochow University and Taipei Language Institute, both in Taiwan. Jeannine was secretary to five HST professors during the five years they lived in Memphis, 1973 – 78. During that time Jeannine developed her language skills beyond the Spanish, French, and Chinese, which she had studied earlier, to include Greek and Hebrew. This prepared her to complete her undergraduate studies. After raising their seven children, she received her B.A. degree in Biblical Languages from Harding University, minor in Chinese, graduating with high honors in 1985.

Jeannine has taught basic Greek to Chinese students, published a song book in Chinese, and currently conducts World English Institute internet studies with students all over the world. The Thweatts established the Christian Service Training

Center in the Tien Mou Community of Taipei, Taiwan, for local Christians in 1983. Later, at the request of young Christians, full-time training in the English language was offered. In addition, daily classes in basic American history and Bible completed the curriculum. This prepared them for study at Christian operated and other universities in the U.S. and other English speaking countries.

Enoch has self-published several booklets; the following have also been translated into Chinese. These were made available mostly for free distribution: *The Search for the True and Living God, What Does "Horse, Horse, Tiger, Tiger" have to do with Understanding Agape Love?, Remembering Jesus,* and *What Did Jesus Build?* He also has published *A Humane Solution to the Illegal Immigration Problem,* but his target audience was too small for general interest; he has withdrawn it from the market.

The Thweatts live in Memphis, Tennessee, where they continue to study and write. They stopped driving at the end of 2018, so were quite accustomed to being "isolated." So, when Covid-19 came along, they were able to take it in stride. They maintain contact with family and friends all over the world by Skype, WhatsApp, Zoom, and other electronic means.

Jeannine has begun to play a dulcimer, and Enoch loves to watch the birds at their feeders. When they want a change from their writing and other responsibilities, they challenge each other to a Domino Train game. Want to join them? Please wear your masks!

Target date for publishing **Beware the Dark Clouds,** book two of **A Trilogy of Clouds** is early Spring, 2021.

CPSIA information can be obtained
at www.ICGtesting.com
Printed in the USA
LVHW030116030221
678172LV00001B/1